ANGELA MOWERY

HERBAL REMEDIES
FOR
BEGINNERS

Discover Herbalism
Naturally With Medicinal
Plants for Everyday
Ailments to Boost Your
Holistic Health, Immunity,
and Wellness

TABLE OF CONTENTS

INTRODUCTION

"An apple a day keeps the doctor away"—does this sound familiar? Well, what if I told you the same goes for herbs? Imagine a world where ancient wisdom meets modern health needs, revealing the power of herbal remedies.

It's a fascinating world but stepping into it can feel daunting. Trust me, I know. During my travels, I saw how different cultures used plants and home remedies, but I didn't delve deeply into it until a chronic illness took over my life. It seemed, in the blink of an eye, that my life was now overshadowed by an illness that controlled every aspect of my day. The constant fatigue, relentless pain, and never-ending doctor's visits had become my new normal. Conventional treatments offered little relief and often came with side effects that left me feeling even worse. I knew I had to find another way, something that would genuinely help me reclaim my life.

That's when I chose to venture further, to see beyond the overwhelming doubts and uncertainties that I'm sure you often feel when faced with challenges, and to explore herbal remedies. Taking a deeper look into herbs and getting overwhelmed by the quality of information at your fingertips is easy. You're not sure what sources to trust, and since it isn't a common route taken when treating one's health, I was bound to be skeptical about whether plants could make a difference. After all, being skeptical was a shield I often used as a form of protection in my life. However, I ventured into this world, ready to explore the hidden caves and secret tunnels in search of knowledge. This knowledge reshaped what I knew and changed how I interacted with my health, leading me to share what I learned with you.

So why should you care about what I have to say? You might ask. Well, it's simple because I'm pretty sure you may desire to take better care of your health, or you're simply intrigued to learn more about health remedies that aren't the traditional methods we're used to. Like me, you're curious about where certain practices came from and yearn for a glimpse of what life was like as far back as 2800 B.C.E. But above all, you want a way to easily understand complex herbal concepts with simplified explanations so that even if you're a complete beginner, you'll be able to grasp them.

With this book, you can effortlessly integrate herbal remedies into your daily life with practical tips and shortcuts that make natural health accessible and convenient. It's the perfect guide as you confidently navigate the world of herbal safety, thanks to quick reference guides and clear safety instructions that demystify the dos and don'ts, ensuring you use remedies effectively and safely.

As you flip through each page, you'll learn to personalize herbal treatments to your specific health needs with easy-to-follow customization techniques that save time and boost effectiveness. You'll overcome common health challenges naturally with simple yet powerful herbal solutions, offering you a natural alternative to conventional treatments. Simultaneously, you'll save time with ready-to-use herbal recipes that provide quick solutions without the need for extensive research or preparation. You'll also make informed decisions with scientifically backed insights that cut through the clutter of misinformation, helping you confidently choose the best herbal remedies for you.

I know it sounds a bit too good to be true, such that the walls of skepticism and distrust might be going up as we speak, but if there's one outcome that is sure to prevail throughout everything, it's the promise of a better life. Imagine waking up feeling refreshed and energized, ready to take on the day with a sense of calm and balance. Instead of reaching for a cup of coffee, you brew a soothing herbal tea that wakes you up gently and supports your overall well-being. As you sip, you feel a connection to nature, and a sense of tranquility washes over you.

Throughout the day, you effortlessly incorporate herbal remedies into your routine. When you feel the midday slump, instead of a sugary snack, you reach for a home-made herbal infusion that revitalizes your energy levels. You carry a small vial of essential oil blend in your bag, ready to calm your nerves before a big meeting or to uplift your mood during a stressful moment.

In the evening, you unwind with a relaxing herbal bath, letting the natural ingredients soothe your muscles and melt away the day's stress. Your skincare routine is simple yet effective, using herb-infused oils that leave your skin glowing and healthy. As you prepare for bed, you take a few drops of a calming herbal tincture that helps you drift off into a deep, restorative sleep.

With herbal remedies, your life feels more harmonious and balanced. You experience fewer colds and minor ailments because your immune system is naturally supported. You feel empowered knowing you can take charge of your health with gentle, effective, and natural solutions. Your home is filled with the delightful scents of dried herbs and essential oils, creating a sanctuary of peace and wellness.

In this new, vibrant life, you move through your days with confidence and ease, knowing that you have the tools to support your health and happiness naturally. Your connection to the earth and its healing gifts brings you joy and fulfillment, making every day a little brighter and more beautiful. This vibrant life is possible because I enjoy experiencing it every day. My experience with chronic illness has given me a deep empathy and understanding of the struggles you might be facing. I've walked in your shoes and have come out the other side with a wealth of knowledge and a renewed zest for life. You are not alone in this journey.

This book isn't just a collection of facts and recipes; it's a guide from someone who's been there and understands the frustration of searching for answers and the joy of finding relief. I've carefully curated the information, ensuring it's practical, easy to understand, and backed by both traditional wisdom and modern science. With this book, you will have the practical tools to take control of your health and well-being.

You can trust that the advice and remedies in this book have been tried and tested by someone who has felt the same despair and hope. Know that, before the wealth of information you're about to dive into, achieving a better life using herbal remedies was no easy feat. The experience was like trying to piece together a puzzle without all the pieces, relying on scattered snippets of knowledge from ancient texts, word-of-mouth traditions, and vague online resources. It was like navigating through a dense forest without a map. However, with this book, you can be confident in the reliability and effectiveness of the information.

In the early days of my journey, I spent countless hours researching, only to find conflicting advice and unverified claims. I would try one remedy after another, often with little to no results and sometimes unexpected side effects. The frustration was immense. I knew there was potential in these natural solutions, but the lack of clear, reliable guidance made it a daunting and often discouraging endeavor.

Back then, understanding which herbs were safe, how to properly prepare them, and how to tailor them to my specific health needs felt like an overwhelming task. There were moments when I wanted to give up, thinking it would be easier to stick with conventional treatments despite their limitations.

Nevertheless, persistence paid off. Through trial and error, I began to piece together effective strategies and reliable information. I connected with knowledgeable herbalists, poured over scientific studies, and experimented with different combinations and preparations. A clearer picture emerged slowly but surely, where herbal remedies could be used safely and effectively to enhance health and well-being.

This book is the culmination of that arduous journey. It's designed to save you from my struggles and provide you with a clear, concise, and comprehensive guide to using herbal remedies. With this information, you'll be able to confidently navigate the world of herbal medicine, avoiding the pitfalls and frustrations that once made it so challenging. Ultimately, your journey, like mine, will become a testament to the healing power of herbal remedies, and I'm here to guide you on your path to better health and well-being. Together, we'll unlock the potential of herbs to transform your life, just as they did mine.

Chapter 1

HISTORICAL ROOTS

Let's get one thing straight: Spending too much time reflecting on your past—unless you're a history buff—is like binge-watching your least favorite show on repeat. It's not very productive and definitely not fun. However, if we're talking about diving into the depths of history, that's a whole different story. Buckle up because we're about to take a fascinating trip to a time when finding a pharmacy was like finding a unicorn and doctors were as scarce as hen's teeth. Let's go back to a time when Mother Nature was the ultimate health guru, and plants were the original prescriptions.

In this chapter, you're about to be transported to a world where people didn't pop pills for their health problems. Instead, they turned to the great green earth for answers, relying on leaves, roots, and flowers to cure what ailed them. It was a time when each plant had its own story and played a vital role in keeping people healthy. Now, it's time to grab your herbal tea, get comfy, and embark on this wild adventure through the annals of ancient healing practices. Trust me, it will be a journey full of surprises, wisdom, and a lot of leafy goodness!

As we traverse these captivating periods, we'll uncover how these ancient practices influence our modern understanding of herbs. Get ready to explore the rich tapestry of herbal history, from Shen Nung's ancient compendium to the aromatic pages of Hippocrates' works and the royal endorsements of King Henry VIII. It's a journey through time that reveals herbs' enduring power and magic.

Evolution of Herbal Medicine Through the Ages

60,000 B.C.E.: Neanderthals and Their Natural Remedies

According to Wild (2023), way back in 60,000 B.C.E., Neanderthals were already onto something with their dental hygiene. Researchers found yarrow, chamomile, and poplar in Neanderthal tooth plaque, proving that plants have been essential for health and nutrition since prehistoric times.

Who knew our caveman ancestors had such sophisticated tastes? Picture them grunting and hunting and chewing on medicinal herbs like early-day herbalists. Forget Flintstone vitamins; these guys were the original natural remedy enthusiasts! Even then, nature was the go-to for a healthier life (and probably fresher breath).

Ancient China, 2800 B.C.E.

In 2800 B.C.E., life was all about simplicity and nature. People lived in close-knit communities, and farming was a big part of daily life. The landscape was dotted with lush fields, and the rivers were the lifeblood of the villages. Here, Shen Nung, also called the "Divine Farmer," made the *Pen-ts'ao*, the first big book of herbs. It lists lots of herbs and what they're good for. He is thought to be the founder of Chinese herbal medicine. Legend says he tasted many herbs to learn how they help, even risking his life in the process.

In the *Pen-ts'ao*, herbs are split into three groups: superior, which are safe for a long time and nontoxic; medium, which might be risky but are helpful in small amounts; and ones that are inferior but can be dangerous, so you should be careful with them.

1500 B.C.E: The Egyptian Ebers Papyrus

In 1500 B.C.E., the Egyptians created the *Ebers Papyrus*, a medical text with over 700 formulas. It's ancient but surprisingly advanced. It describes the circulatory system and recognizes blood vessels and the heart's function. It includes herbs like aloe, basil, and bayberry, which are still popular today.

Greece, 400 B.C.E.

Now, let's fast-forward to 400 B.C.E. in Greece. Everyone's strutting around in togas, chatting about philosophy like it's the latest gossip. Socrates is on the street corner, questioning everything under the sun. Amid this intellectual buzz, we find ourselves enveloped by the aromatic symphony of herbs. Hippocrates, the wise healer, is busy documenting the first Greek herbal, capturing the essence of sage and thyme. His works pass down ancient herbal wisdom through the ages, ensuring these secrets aren't lost.

100 B.C.E.: Illustrated Herbal Manuscripts in Greece

For visual learners, back in those days, you'd give thanks to the Greeks as they pioneered the creation of illustrated herbal manuscripts. These manuscripts contained detailed drawings and descriptions of medicinal plants to serve as visual guides for herbalists and physicians.

50: Herbal Knowledge in the Roman Empire

By 50, the Roman Empire had spread herbal medicine across its vast territories, incorporating knowledge from the regions they conquered. During this time, Dioscorides, a Roman physician, also wrote *De Materia Medica*, a comprehensive herbal text that remained influential for centuries. The Romans established extensive trade routes, bringing exotic plants and herbs from distant lands into the empire. Public baths often used aromatic herbs in the water to promote hygiene and health, while wealthy Romans grew medicinal herbs in their gardens, blending leisure with health practices. Even though the Roman Empire is famous for its architecture and fierce army, their use and development of herbs have impacted Europe.

23–79: Pliny the Elder and "Natural History"

Pliny the Elder, a Roman polymath, wrote *Natural History* between 23 and 79, cataloging over 900 drugs and plants. He believed in the mystical properties of plants like mandrake, which he said screamed when pulled from the ground—a scream that could be deadly talk about a dramatic plant.

126–216: Galen's Contributions to Roman Medicine

Between 126 and 216, Galen made significant contributions to Roman medicine by categorizing illnesses and herbal remedies. He also discovered that arteries carry blood, which was a pretty big deal.

500: The Physicians of Myddfai in Medieval Wales

In 500, the physicians of Myddfai in Wales practiced holistic healing, emphasizing diet, exercise, and herbal remedies. Their approach reflected a deep connection to nature and its healing properties. It's safe to say they were the original wellness influencers!

800: European Monasteries as Herbal Sanctuaries

By 800, European monasteries had become centers of herbal knowledge. Monks cultivated physic gardens, essentially outdoor apothecaries, where medicinal plants thrived alongside spiritual contemplation. Imagine monks in robes tending to their herbal remedies.

1098–1179: Hildegard of Bingen

Between 1098 and 1179, Hildegard of Bingen, a Benedictine nun, wrote *Causae et Curae* and *Physica*. These works highlighted the prominence of herbalism among women in Germanic tribes. Hildegard was a mystic, writer, and composer, paving the way for women in various fields, making her what many of us would deem, in this day and age, the ultimate girl boss.

1100: Avicenna and the Canon of Medicine

In 1100, Avicenna (Ibn Sina) emerged in Persia, bridging ancient and medieval medical traditions with his *Canon of Medicine*. He drew on Persian, Greek, Indian, and Arabic knowledge, making him the original medical influencer.

1200: The Black Death and Herbal Remedies

During the 1200s, the Black Death, which was as terrifying as it sounds, swept through Europe. Apothecaries and herbalists both struggled to find effective treatments. The quest for remedies spurred much experimentation, with herbalists at the forefront scrambling in a frantic race for a cure.

1500: Henry VIII and Herbal Medicine

A man known to have six wives whose fates were often summarized in the rhyme, "Divorced, beheaded, died;

divorced, beheaded, survived," he supported the use of herbs. His support contributed to the advancement of herbal medicine in England, laying the groundwork for more study of medicinal plants.

1545–1612: John Gerard and the Elizabethan Era

In the Elizabethan era, John Gerard, a curious botanist, roamed the fragrant meadows of England and wrote *The Herbal or General History of Plants*. His work left a lasting mark on English herbalism, capturing the growing fascination with nature. Imagine him as the original plant geek, scribbling down secrets of the garden.

1600: Nicholas Culpeper's Revolution

By 1600, society had a two-tier health system: herbs for the poor and exotic treatments for the rich. Enter Nicholas Culpeper, the herbalist rebel who wrote *The English Physician* and *The Complete Herbal*. He challenged the elite medical world by making herbal knowledge accessible to everyone. Think of him as the people's herbalist, simplifying remedies for the commoners.

1800: A Shift to Synthetic Drugs

The 19th century saw a shift to synthetic drugs like mercury and laudanum, which were sold over the counter. With serious side effects becoming common, the booming pharmaceutical industry made herbal medicine seem outdated. It was like herbal remedies got kicked to the curb by the cool new kids in town.

1822–1913: Harriet Tubman, Herbalist and Hero

Harriet Tubman, born into slavery, became a symbol of liberation and a guardian of herbal wisdom. After escaping slavery, she rescued around 70 people through the Underground Railroad. Known as the "Moses of Her People," Tubman was also a skilled herbalist, using her knowledge as a Union nurse during the Civil War. She was a real-life superhero with a green thumb.

1864–1943: George Washington Carver, Plant Pioneer

George Washington Carver, born into slavery, was a pioneering agricultural scientist and herbalist. At the Tuskegee Institute, his experiments with peanuts and sweet potatoes extended to medicinal plants. His lab could truly be described as a modern-day magic workshop, creating herbal remedies for the community. Carver was all about sustainable agriculture and keeping the soil healthy.

1900: The Rise of Pharmaceuticals

By 1900, scientists were isolating and altering plant compounds to create synthetic drugs, further displacing herbal medicine. However, about 25% of today's pharmaceutical drugs still have botanical origins. After World War I, the pharmaceutical industry exploded, and herbalists faced new challenges. The Pharmacy and Medicines Act of 1941 tried to limit herbalists, but public outcry kept the tradition alive.

2000: Herbal Medicine in the Modern World

In 2000, European legislation called for clinical testing of all herbal medicines, similar to conventional drugs. Despite this, the U.K. government refused to regulate herbal medicines in 2015. Today, herbalism survives thanks to dedicated herbalists and public support. The World Health Organization estimates that 80% of people globally use herbal medicines for primary healthcare. However, it's less than 12% in the UK. Recently, dissatisfaction with prescription costs and a love for natural remedies have sparked a resurgence in herbal medicine, especially in the US and UK.

Approaches to Herbalism Across the Globe

Herbal medicine is not only a Western practice but a global one, seamlessly intertwined with culture and tradition worldwide. We'll take a brief look at five different cultural approaches to herbalism. Although plants are used universally, each culture has its unique spin on using them.

South African Herbal Medicine

Among the Zulu tribe of South Africa, traditional healers known as "inyanga" have long practiced herbal medicine, utilizing the rich array of indigenous plants to address numerous ailments. For instance, if you need stomach pain relief, using the African potato (*Hypoxis hemerocallidea*) for its anti-inflammatory properties and wild ginger for digestive issues are your answer and are a glimpse of the herbal knowledge woven throughout the tribe's culture.

Chinese Herbal Medicine

Chinese herbal medicine is all about balancing yin and yang—maintaining harmony between the forces of light and dark. Plants like ginseng and astragalus are rock stars in this system, helping to keep everything in sync. Here, health is about more than just feeling good physically—it's also about spiritual and emotional well-being.

Egyptian Herbalism

The ancient Egyptians saw plants as sacred healers. Their famous *Ebers Papyrus*, a medical text from 1500 B.C.E., shows how they used plants like aloe vera and garlic to treat both body and soul. They believed in a strong connection between nature and well-being, making their approach to health holistic.

Native American Herbal Practices

Native American tribes used herbal remedies as part of their spiritual beliefs. Plants like sage and sweetgrass were used in healing and ceremonies, showing their deep connection to nature. For them, health was a mix of physical well-being and spiritual harmony. It's like they had the ultimate nature-based health plan.

Unani Tibb Practices

Unani Tibb, a type of Persio-Arabic medicine, focuses on balancing bodily humors or body fluids. Plants like black cumin and licorice root are key players here, used to restore balance and keep everything in check. Health in this system is all about keeping the body's humors in perfect proportion, like a well-mixed cocktail.

Comparing Ancient and Modern Practices

Western herbalism draws from these ancient systems, mixing old wisdom with new science. This blend creates a rich tapestry of healing practices that have evolved. Let's dive into some key points:

Use of Natural Products

From ancient times to today, nature's pharmacy—plants, animals, microorganisms, and marine life—has been a constant source of remedies. Whether in ancient apothecaries or modern herbalists' shops, these natural products are central to healing.

Holistic Approach

Ancient and modern herbal practices share a holistic approach to health, viewing well-being as more than just the absence of disease. They emphasize the interconnectedness of physical, mental, and spiritual health, ensuring a comprehensive understanding of well-being.

Clinical Experiences

Both ancient and modern herbalists rely on extensive clinical experience. Traditional systems developed precise dosage, preparation, and harvesting methods that align with modern evidence-based practices.

Contribution to Modern Medicine

Many modern medicines have roots in traditional herbal knowledge. About 40% of pharmaceuticals come from natural sources. For example, aspirin and artemisinin were inspired by ancient herbal remedies.

Global Use

Herbal medicine transcends geographical boundaries, thriving alongside modern medical practices. Chinese, Indian, and European herbal traditions continue to flourish, demonstrating the universal appeal of plant-based healing.

Regulation and Quality Control

Ensuring the safety and efficacy of remedies has always been crucial. While ancient herbalists used meticulous observation and passed-down knowledge, today's herbal medicine follows strict international regulations and quality control standards.

Treating Different Ailments

Herbal medicine has been used for a wide range of health issues, from allergies and asthma to chronic fatigue and even cancer. Ancient herbalists treated many ailments, and today's herbalists continue this tradition, often alongside modern medical treatments.

Looking Ahead: Embracing an Herbal Future

Herbalism connects the past with the present, blending ancient wisdom with modern knowledge. Using nature's gifts for healing, considering the whole person, and contributing to overall health show how herbal medicine has evolved. Looking back and forth, we see how old and new practices can lead to better health.

Reflecting on our journey with plants, we see the historical roots of herbal medicine. From ancient China's earliest records to medieval Europe's pioneering herbalists, this story is one of resilience, wisdom, and the ongoing importance of herbal remedies. Every plant had a purpose, and every remedy carried a legacy. The cultural significance of herbal practices is evident, from the Chinese yin-yang balance to Native American spiritual connections. Figures like Hippocrates and Culpeper have left lasting marks on herbal medicine, shaping its path through history.

With this historical foundation, consider adding herbalism to your daily routine. Start by trying herbal teas, exploring natural remedies for common issues, or even starting a small herb garden. Herbalism isn't just about looking back; it's about actively engaging with the healing power of plants today and incorporating them into your life.

In the next chapter, we'll dive into the world of herbs. We'll explore their classifications and benefits, giving you a clear understanding of how these natural healers can improve your life. We'll examine their properties, uses, and how ancient knowledge fits into modern herbal remedies. Get ready to meet the green allies that have stood the test of time and learn how they can boost your well-being. Nature's remedies are waiting to be discovered!

Chapter 2

ESSENCE DISCOVERY

In the enormous world of herbal remedies, a special garden filled with plants can help your body heal. Welcome to this garden of healing, where every leaf and flower holds secrets to treating various health problems. We'll explore well-known herbs like lavender and less familiar but just as powerful ones. By the end of this chapter, you'll be able to recognize different herbs, understand their benefits, and appreciate the science behind these natural cures.

Entering the World of Herbs: A Simple Guide to Classification

Exploring the fascinating world of herbs means understanding how they are organized. Organizing by plant classification helps us identify and learn about the many different kinds of medicinal plants.

Basic Classification

Herbs are categorized based on their botanical characteristics, which helps herbalists and enthusiasts alike. Here's a simplified version of how herbs are classified:

Kingdom

- Plantae: All herbs are part of the plant kingdom.

Division or Phylum

- Magnoliophyta: This group includes flowering plants, such as basil (Ocimum basilicum).

Class

- Magnoliopsida: Many herbs fall into this class. Oregano (*Origanum vulgare*) is one of them.

Order

- Lamiales: In this order, you'll find herbs like mint (*Mentha*), including varieties like peppermint (*Mentha × piperita*).

Family

- Lamiaceae (mint Family): This family includes herbs such as rosemary (*Salvia rosmarinus*).

Genus

- *Salvia*: This genus includes herbs like sage (*Salvia officinalis*) and clary sage (*Salvia sclarea*).

Species

- *Lavandula angustifolia*: This is the specific species for lavender.

Common Species Names

- "Vulgaris": This term often means the plant is common or found in the wild. For instance, oregano is called *Origanum vulgare*.

- "Officinalis": This term is linked to plants with known medicinal uses. Sage, for example, is *Salvia officinalis*, indicating its traditional medicinal role.

Why Understanding Taxonomy Matters

- **Accurate identification:** Using scientific names helps herbalists correctly identify plants.

- **Clear communication:** Communication is always key, and consistent naming ensures that everyone refers to the same plant, reducing confusion.

- **Historical use:** The term "officinalis" points to plants with a history of medicinal use, which can be important for therapeutic purposes.

Herb classification provides a systematic way to organize and understand these plants, making it easier for anyone to understand. By knowing their scientific names and classifications, herbalists can communicate clearly and ensure they use the correct plants for their needs.

Plant Parts Used in Herbal Remedies

Understanding which parts of the plant hold the medicinal magic is crucial. Different parts of the plant have unique benefits. Let's break it down to get an accurate and complete picture of each part and its function.

Leaves

- Example: Basil and mint

- Fun fact: Leaves are like the overachievers of the herb world. They're always packed with flavor and medicinal goodness. Who knew being green could be so powerful?

Flowers

- Example: Chamomile and lavender

- Fun fact: Flowers are the drama queens of plants—they look pretty and have all the healing properties, perfect for when you need some pet-al-powered relaxation.

Roots

- Example: Ginseng and turmeric
- Fun fact: Roots are the underground superhe-roes. They might look like gnarled sticks, but as they say, "Never judge a book by its cover," these roots are good for storing up all the good stuff.

Seeds

- Example: Coriander and fennel
- Fun fact: Seeds are tiny but mighty. Packed with essential oils and nutrients, they're like the pock-et-sized dynamo of the plant world. Great things come in small packages.

Bark

- Example: Willow bark
- Fun fact: Bark is the tough guy, the plant's suit of armor. Like any tough guy, it has a soft side—like containing salicin, which helps relieve pain. This makes tree bark a surprisingly soothing part.

Berries

- Example: Elderberries and juniper berries
- Fun fact: Berries are like the fun, fruity sidekicks that taste great and boost your health. It's like nature's way of giving you a healthy snack and medicine all in one.

As we navigate the classifications, remember that many herbs can be part of multiple categories in nature's pharmacy, making them versatile and ready to im-press. Understanding the different parts of herbs and their uses is like unlocking the secret menu at a fancy restaurant—each part brings something unique to the table!

Properties of Herbs

Therapeutic Properties

Herbalists use special terms to describe what herbs do for your body. These terms help them discuss how different herbs can help with specific health issues. Let's break down some of these terms.

Alteratives

- What they do: Slowly restore the body's proper function and boost overall health

- Examples: Burdock and red clover

- Fun fact: Alteratives are the herb world's slow and steady personal trainers—they help you get in shape over time.

Adaptogens

- What they do: Help the body handle stress and get back to normal

- Examples: Ginseng and holy basil

- Fun fact: Adaptogens are like your chill friends, who always know how to keep you calm and collected, no matter what life throws at you.

Nervines

- What they do: Benefit the nervous system, often with calming effects

- Examples: Lavender and chamomile

- Fun fact: Nervines are the soothing lullabies of herbs—perfect for winding down after a long day.

Diuretics

- What they do: Help the body get rid of excess fluids by making you pee more
- Examples: Dandelion and parsley
- Fun fact: Diuretics are the body's natural plumbers and help flush out what you don't need.

Antispasmodics

- What they do: Relieve spasms or cramps
- Examples: peppermint and valerian root
- Fun fact: These herbs are like the masseuses of the plant world, easing annoying cramps and spasms and reducing tension in your body.

Astringents

- What they do: Cause tissues to contract and shrink, often used to stop bleeding
- Examples: Witch hazel and yarrow
- Fun fact: Astringents tighten things up and stop the leaks. Think of them as housekeepers who tidy things up in the plant world.

Bitters

- What they do: Stimulate the digestive system by triggering bitter receptors
- Examples: Gentian and dandelion root
- Fun fact: Bitters reminds me of those friends who give you tough love. Sure, they won't give you what you want, but they give you what you need

and get your digestive system running smoothly despite their bitter taste.

Demulcents

- What they do: Soothe and protect mucous membranes with a protective film
- Examples: Marshmallow and slippery elm
- Fun fact: Demulcents are gentle caregivers, coating and comforting your insides like a warm hug.

Scientists have identified several other key properties of herbs that contribute to their overall utility and benefits, in addition to the therapeutic benefits offered by herbs. Here's a simplified overview based on information from various scientific sources.

Culinary Properties

- Flavor enhancement: Some herbs add delicious flavors to our food.
- Example: Herbs like basil, oregano, and thyme
- Fun fact: With dandelion (yes, the weed), for instance, the young leaves add a peppery taste to a salad. Some herbs make everything taste gourmet, which would certainly put you on track to becoming the next Gordon Ramsey.

Nutritional Properties

- Vitamins and minerals: Many herbs are packed with essential nutrients.
- Examples: Parsley is rich in vitamin C, and spinach provides iron.
- Fun fact: Herbs are like tiny multivitamins growing in your garden!

Aromatic Properties

- Fragrance: Some herbs are known for the pleasant scents they offer.

- Example: Herbs such as lavender, rosemary, and mint

- Fun fact: They're natural air fresheners, making your space smell delightful.

Antimicrobial Properties

- Fighting germs: Some herbs have natural compounds that can kill or inhibit the growth of bacteria and fungi.

- Examples: Garlic and thyme are known for their antimicrobial effects.

- Fun fact: These herbs are like the bouncers of the plant world, kicking out unwanted microbial guests who are trying to spoil the fun for everybody.

Antioxidant Properties

- Free radical scavenging: Contains antioxidants that protect cells from damage

- Example: Herbs like rosemary and oregano

- Fun fact: They're like superheroes fighting off evil free radicals.

Insecticidal Properties

- Pest control: Some herbs can repel insects.

- Examples: Basil and citronella are commonly used to keep bugs at bay.

- Fun fact: They're your garden's natural bug repellent.

Ornamental Properties

- Aesthetic appeal: Many herbs are grown for their beauty.

- Examples: Lavender and ornamental sage are popular in gardens for their looks.

- Fun fact: These herbs are the supermodels of the plant kingdom, adding beauty wherever they grow.

Understanding these diverse properties highlights the multifaceted benefits of herbs, making them indispensable in various aspects of life. Whether adding flavor to our meals, improving our health, or making our surroundings more pleasant, herbs genuinely are nature's little miracles.

Common Herbs and Their Healing Properties

- Let's explore some well-known herbs, their healing benefits, and how to easily use them daily.

Lavender

- Benefits: Lavender helps you relax, reduce stress, and sleep better. It also has antimicrobial and antioxidant properties.

- How to use: Diffuse lavender oil in your home, put dried lavender in sachets for a calming scent in your closet, or make lavender tea to drink before bed.

Chamomile

- Benefits: Chamomile, with its delicate daisy-like flowers, reduces inflammation, aids digestion, and helps you sleep. It can also soothe skin irritations when applied topically and is known to enhance the natural highlights in blonde hair when used as a rinse, lending a touch of sun-kissed radiance to your locks.

- How to use: Drink chamomile tea before bed, use chamomile-infused skincare products, or take chamomile capsules for nausea relief.

Peppermint

- Benefits: Peppermint eases indigestion, has antimicrobial properties, and can help with headaches and concentration.

- How to use: Drink peppermint tea after meals for digestion, inhale peppermint oil for an energy boost, or add fresh peppermint leaves to salads or drinks for flavor.

Echinacea

- Benefits: Echinacea is beloved for its immune-boosting properties and was once used by Native American tribes as a toothache remedy. It helps prevent colds and infections and has wound-healing properties. It may also reduce the severity of cold symptoms.

- How to use: Make echinacea tea, use echinacea tinctures during the cold season, or infuse honey with echinacea for an immunity boost.

Feverfew

- Benefits: Feverfew, touted for its potential to alleviate migraines, has an interesting claim to fame in folklore. It was once believed that planting feverfew by the doorstep would ward off witches, which is fascinating. It is also helpful for fevers.

- How to use: Drink feverfew tea regularly, add fresh leaves to salads, or take feverfew supplements for migraine prevention.

Garlic

- Benefits: Garlic has antimicrobial, heart-protective, and anti-inflammatory properties. It may help with heart health, cholesterol, and cancer prevention.

- How to use: Add raw garlic to salads, make garlic-infused olive oil for cooking, or take garlic supplements for specific health goals. I suggest mixing garlic with honey. Adding honey is a great way to take in the bitter-tasting herbs. Beware that the honey and garlic mixture may turn blue due to the sulfur compounds in the garlic. It is perfectly fine, however.

Ginger

- Benefits: Ginger eases nausea and motion sickness and helps with pregnancy-related or chemotherapy-induced nausea. In addition to these medical benefits, it's renowned for offering a spicy kick in culinary and is a natural breath freshener.

- How to use: Drink ginger tea, add grated ginger to smoothies, or take ginger supplements or candies for nausea relief.

Ginkgo

- Benefits: Ginkgo trees are resilient and live for over 1,000 years. This herb treats asthma, bronchitis, fatigue, and tinnitus. It may also improve memory and help prevent dementia.

- How to use: Take ginkgo supplements, drink ginkgo-infused beverages, or add ginkgo leaves to salads.

Ginseng

- Benefits: Ginseng is used as a tonic, aphrodisiac, and cure-all for cognitive functions and stress. Its effectiveness varies, so it is important to source high-quality products.

- How to use: Drink ginseng tea, take capsules, and choose reputable ginseng products.

Goldenseal

- Benefits: Goldenseal treats diarrhea and eye and skin irritations. Its berberine content is medicinal.

- How to use: Make a goldenseal eyewash, take goldenseal supplements, or use goldenseal-infused creams.

Milk Thistle

- Benefits: Milk thistle treats liver conditions and high cholesterol and may reduce cancer cell growth.

- How to use: Take milk thistle supplements or use them in recipes like soups, salads, and stews.

St. John's Wort

- Benefits: St. John's wort is used as an antidepressant, especially for mild to moderate depression. Interestingly, this herb has a long history of folklore and superstition surrounding its ability to ward off evil spirits and protect against negative energy.

- How to use: Take St. John's wort supplements, make an infusion with dried St. John's wort, and consult a healthcare professional about potential interactions with other medications.

Saw Palmetto

- Benefits: Saw palmetto is used for urinary symptoms related to benign prostatic hyperplasia (BPH), though its effectiveness is debatable. The berries were also thought to have aphrodisiac properties and were sometimes included in rituals by Native American tribes for fertility.

- How to use: Take saw palmetto supplements, add berries to smoothies, and consult a healthcare professional about side effects and interactions.

Valerian

- Benefits: Valerian helps with sleep and reduces anxiety. Although herbs offer numerous benefits to humans, valerian has a unique attraction to cats, acting as a natural sedative for them. Cats can't help but be drawn to the scent of valerian root, often exhibiting playful and relaxed behavior when exposed to it, which is a helpful tip for all the cat owners out there.

- How to use: For a calming bedtime routine, drink Valerian tea before bed, take Valerian supplements, or use Valerian-infused oils.

Exploration of Uncommon Herbs and Their Unique Benefits

These herbs may be less popular, but they have unique healing properties and are worth exploring.

Ashwagandha (Indian Ginseng)

- Benefits: Ashwagandha calms you, reduces inflammation, and boosts vitality.

- How to use: Drink ashwagandha tea or take supplements for relaxation and energy.

Brahmi (Nature's Stress Reliever)

- Benefits: Brahmi reduces anxiety and stress and relieves stomach pain.

- How to use: Add Brahmi to teas or use it in skin-care for its calming effects.

Epazote (Bean Dish Companion)

- Benefits: Epazote reduces gas from bean dishes.

- How to use: Add epazote to your bean recipes for better digestion.

Holy Basil (Sacred Healing)

- Benefits: Holy basil, or tulsi, treats colds, flu, respiratory infections, and general aches and relieves stress.

- How to use: Drink tulsi tea or take supplements to boost your health.

Marshmallow (Beyond the Snack)

- Benefits: Marshmallow soothes inflammation and irritation, soothing for sore throats.

- How to use: Make marshmallow tea, tincture it, or use it in skincare for its soothing effects.

Mullein (Lung Guardian)

- Benefits: Mullein helps with respiratory issues like coughs and laryngitis.

- How to use: Brew mullein tea, tincture it, or use it in herbal remedies for lung health.

Growing these uncommon herbs might require more effort, often requiring trusted online sources. As you explore these herbal treasures, you'll find their unique benefits, which add depth to your herbal collection and expand your natural remedy tool kit.

Scientific Research Supporting Herbal Benefits

It would be adequate to say that herbs are nature's little helpers that have been getting lots of love from science lately. Beyond the aesthetic appeal, they have many benefits that make them more than just the pretty face we see. From making us feel good to keeping us healthy, herbs have our backs in more ways than one.

Picture this: Traditional wisdom meets modern research in a buddy cop movie where the herbs are the stars. When science puts these plants under the microscope, it's like giving them an upgrade that elevates them to a higher level. Suddenly, those old herbal remedies aren't just folklore but real, scientifically backed powerhouses.

Test Your Knowledge

Now, let's shake things up with a quiz! Think you know your herbs? Match them up with their benefits and see if you've got what it takes to be an herbal expert. It's like Tinder for herbs (without the possibility of an awkward date).

1. Herb: Mullein

   a. Helps with respiratory issues

   b. Reduces inflammation

   c. Enhances memory

   d. Promotes sleep

2. Herb: Ginger

   a. Lowers blood sugar

   b. Aids in digestion and relieves nausea

   c. Boosts immunity

   d. Improves skin health

3. Herb: Peppermint

   a. Relieves headaches and improves concentration

   b. Reduces joint pain

   c. Enhances liver function

   d. Promotes weight loss

4. Herb: Echinacea

   a. Supports the immune system

   b. Reduces anxiety

   c. Lowers cholesterol

   d. Aids in digestion

5. Herb: Ginseng

   a. Enhances cognitive function and reduces stress

   b. Lowers blood pressure

   c. Relieves pain

   d. Improves eyesight

6. Herb: Chamomile

   a. Enhances athletic performance

   b. Reduces anxiety and promotes sleep

   c. Improves bone health

   d. Boosts metabolism

7. Herb: Holy Basil

   a. Improves heart health

   b. Boosts hair growth

   c. Supports the immune system and reduces stress

   d. Reduces symptoms of arthritis

8. Herb: Garlic

   a. Enhances libido

   b. Improves cardiovascular health

   c. Reduces inflammation

   d. Promotes digestive health

9. Herb: Lavender

   a. Reduces stress and improves sleep quality

   b. Enhances skin health

   c. Aids in weight loss

   d. Boosts immune function

10. Herb: Marshmallow

    a. Soothes sore throat and cough

    b. Improves brain function and memory

    c. Relieves constipation

    d. Reduces menstrual pain

Answers

1. B) Reduces inflammation
2. B) Aids in digestion and relieves nausea
3. A) Relieves headaches and improves concentration
4. A) Supports the immune system
5. A) Enhances cognitive function and reduces stress
6. B) Reduces anxiety and promotes sleep
7. C) Enhances memory and concentration
8. B) Improves cardiovascular health
9. A) Reduces stress and improves sleep quality
10. A) Soothes sore throat and cough

Winding Down

After deep diving into this chapter, we've discovered popular herbs like lavender and chamomile. We even peeked at the underdogs and their secret healing abilities. After everything is said and done, it's safe to say science is on our side, supporting herbs.

Armed with knowledge and a sprinkle of herbal magic, why not spice up your life with a dose of herb action? Brew herbal teas, sniff some essential oils, or start your mini herb kingdom. There's a whole universe out there waiting for you to explore.

In the next chapter, we'll debunk some herbal myths together. Get ready to sort the real from the fake news and level up your herbal IQ. It's time to separate the parsley from the sage and become a certified herb aficionado. Are you excited? Let's do this!

Chapter 3

REALITY CHECK

Have you ever heard that herbal remedies are just old wives' tales or are a cure-all for every ailment? This chapter will explore and clear up the truths and confusion about herbal medicine. I admit I once believed in certain misunderstandings about herbs before I began researching that world in depth. For instance, when I learned that there were plants that could help with colds and coughs, I thought they would taste like grass, but that's far from the truth. They all have different flavors, but I have not yet encountered one that tastes like grass. Thus, it's essential to clarify the often-confusing world of herbal remedies and dismantle any fears you may have.

Common Myths Versus Facts About Herbal Remedies

Myth 1: Herbal Medicine Isn't Backed by Research

Fact: Many studies show that herbal remedies can work. Modern science is constantly investigating and confirming what herbs can do. People have been using them successfully for hundreds of years, so they have some serious credibility.

Myth 2: I Can't Take Herbal Medicine If I'm on Prescription Meds

Fact: While herbs and drugs can sometimes clash, the trick is to tell your herbalist and doctor about everything you're taking. With good communication, herbal and regular treatments can often work together like a dream team.

Myth 3: Herbal Medicine Is Natural, So It's Always Safe

Fact: Just because something is natural doesn't mean it's safe. Herbs can have side effects, and their safety depends on how much you take, your health, and how they mix with other meds.

Myth 4: Herbs Must Be Taken for Weeks or Months Before They Work

Fact: Some herbs work quickly, while others need time to show results. It depends on the herb and what it's supposed to do. Knowing what to expect can help you be more patient (or not).

Myth 5: Herbal Medicine Is Expensive

Fact: Herbal remedies can be cheaper than pharmaceuticals, especially over time. Growing or buying your herbs in bulk can save you even more money. Plus, it's fun to have your own little herb garden. At least this way, you know where the herbs came from, how they were grown, etc.

Myth 6: Herbal Medicine Is the Same as Homeopathy

Fact: Nope, they're different. Herbal medicine uses plants, while homeopathy uses tiny amounts of natural substances diluted many times. Knowing the difference helps you make better choices.

Myth 7: Herbal Remedies Can Cure Any Illness

Fact: Herbal remedies can benefit certain conditions but are not a cure-all. They are best used to complement conventional treatments, not replace them.

Myth 8: All Herbal Remedies Are Effective

Fact: The effectiveness of herbal remedies varies. Some herbs have been scientifically proven effective for specific conditions, while others lack sufficient evidence. For example, echinacea is often used to prevent colds, but studies have shown mixed results regarding its effectiveness.

Myth 9: More Is Better When It Comes to Herbal Remedies

Fact: Taking more than the recommended dose of an herbal remedy can be harmful. Like conventional medications, herbs can have toxic effects if taken in excessive amounts.

By debunking these myths, I hope to provide you with a clearer understanding of herbal remedies' real benefits and limitations. Always consult a healthcare professional before starting any new treatment, herbal or otherwise.

Herbs Without Harm: The Happy Herbalist's Guide to Safe Herbal Medicine

In this part of the book, you'll discover how to safely harness the power of plants to enhance your health and well-being through some key steps that have been researched and that I've personally found helpful in my herbal journey.

Step 1: Know Thy Herbs—A Beginner's Guide

Before you dive headfirst into the herbal jungle, it's crucial to familiarize yourself with your leafy friends. Here are some tips to get started:

1.1. Identify Your Herbs

Not all green things are good for you. Make sure you're picking parsley and not poison hemlock. Use reputable sources for plant identification, like books, apps, or your local botany club.

1.2. Start With the Basics

Begin with well-known and widely used herbs such as chamomile, peppermint, and ginger. These herbs are like the vanilla ice cream of the herbal world—simple, safe, and almost universally loved.

Step 2: Dosage—Because Size Matters

Herbs can be potent, so getting the dose right is critical.

2.1. Tinctures and Teas

A typical dose for tinctures is 1–2 dropperfuls, while for teas, 1–2 teaspoons of dried herb per cup of hot water will suffice. Always start with the lower end of the dosage range—it's better to be safe than sing the blues from the bathroom.

2.2. Capsules and Tablets

These are often standardized, meaning they contain a specific amount of active ingredients. Follow the instructions on the label. If the label says to take two and you think more is better, remember: it's medicine, not a buffet!

Step 3: Interactions and Side Effects—The Fine Print

Herbs can interact with medications and other herbs, so knowing the potential side effects is important.

3.1. Common Interactions

St. John's wort, for instance, is the life of the party but doesn't play well with antidepressants, birth control pills, or blood thinners. Think of it as the herbal equivalent of that friend who can't hold their liquor.

3.2. Allergic Reactions

If you're allergic to a particular plant family (like ragweed), you might also react to related herbs (like chamomile). When trying a new herb, start with a small amount to see how your body reacts.

Step 4: Sourcing and Storing Your Herbs—Keeping It Fresh

Freshness matters in the world of herbs.

4.1. Sourcing

Buy from reputable suppliers. If you're foraging, ensure you're in an area free from pesticides and pollution. Farmer's markets are a good place, and you might make a friend who grows rosemary. Besides buying from reputable suppliers, I would grow some herbs and avoid using chemicals. Creating your little herb paradise in the yard is also a good route.

4.2. Storing

Store dried herbs in a cool, dark place in airtight containers. Fresh herbs can be stored in the fridge like the leftover salad you swear you will eat tomorrow.

Step 5: Consult the Experts—You're Not Alone

Just because it's natural doesn't mean it's always safe for everyone.

5.1. Talk to Your Doctor

Always consult with a healthcare professional before starting any new herbal regimen, especially if you're pregnant, nursing, or have a chronic condition. Think of your doctor as your health sidekick, always ready to swoop in if things get tricky.

5.2. Herbalists and Naturopaths

Seek advice from certified herbalists or naturopaths. They've spent years learning how to harness the power of herbs safely, so don't hesitate to ask them for guidance.

Understanding the Limitations and Realistic Expectations

Herbal remedies have been praised for their health benefits for a long time. However, it's important to know their limits. Let's take a closer look at why herbs aren't magical cures and why keeping your expectations realistic is crucial. One significant limitation of herbal remedies is that they aren't strictly regulated like prescription drugs. Here's what that means for you:

- **Lack of standardization:** Unlike medications, herbs don't have strict rules about how they're made. This means that the strength and quality can vary from one product to another.

- **Limited research:** While some herbs have been studied and shown to work, many have not. This lack of research means we don't always know how effective or safe they are.

- **Consistency and reliability:** Because herbal products aren't closely regulated, you might get a high-quality product one time and a lower-quality one the next. This inconsistency can make it hard to know what you're really getting.

While herbal remedies can be beneficial, it's important to understand their limitations. They are not cure-alls, and the lack of strict regulations means you must be careful about your chosen products. Always keep realistic expectations and do your research to use herbs safely and effectively.

Potential Side Effects: What to Watch Out For

When using herbs, you must keep your expectations realistic and be aware of possible side effects. Here's what you need to know:

Common Side Effects

Even the most popular herbs can cause side effects. Here's a quick rundown of what to keep in mind:

- **Stomach upset:** Some herbs, like peppermint, can cause stomach irritation or heartburn, especially if taken in large amounts.

- **Allergic reactions:** Just like with food, you might be allergic to some herbs. Watch for signs like itching, rash, or difficulty breathing.

- **Drowsiness:** Herbs like valerian root can make you sleepy. This is great for bedtime, but not so much if you need to drive or operate heavy machinery.

- **Photosensitivity:** St. John's wort can make your skin more sensitive to sunlight, increasing the risk of sunburn.

Serious Side Effects

While rare, some herbs can cause more severe health issues:

- **Liver damage:** Herbs like kava and comfrey are linked to long-term liver problems.

- **Kidney problems:** Some herbs, such as juniper, can be harsh on the kidneys if used excessively.

- **Heart issues:** Ephedra, also known as ma huang, can cause heart palpitations and high blood pressure. It's best to avoid this one unless under professional supervision.

Herb Interactions: The Herbal–Drug Dance—Complex Interactions

Mixing herbs with prescription meds can be like mixing up dance partners. Sometimes it works; sometimes it doesn't. These herbal–drug interactions can change how your medications work or make side effects worse. It's like adding an unexpected dance move that throws off the whole routine.

So be careful and exercise a lot of caution when roaming a world where these two mix. Although there are many benefits to herbs, it's important to avoid wearing rose-colored glasses when it comes to the potential dangers of mixing them with other medications. Here are a few examples:

- **Blood thinners:** Garlic, ginger, and ginkgo can thin your blood. If you're on blood-thinning medication like warfarin, taking these herbs could increase your risk of bleeding.

- **Antidepressants:** St. John's wort can interfere with antidepressants, potentially causing a condition known as serotonin syndrome, which can be life-threatening.

- **Blood pressure meds:** Licorice root can raise blood pressure, so avoid it if you're taking medication for high blood pressure.

Tips for Safe Herbal Use

- **Start small:** When trying a new herb, start with a small dose to see how your body reacts.

- **Consult a professional:** Always talk to a health-care provider or a certified herbalist before adding herbs to your routine, especially if you're taking other medications.

- **Do your research:** Use reputable sources to learn about herbs and their potential effects. Reliable websites include the National Center for Complementary and Integrative Health (NCCIH) and Mayo Clinic.

- **Monitor your health:** Track any new symptoms or side effects and report them to your health-care provider immediately.

Herbs can be a fantastic way to support your health, but they're not without risks. You can use herbs safely and effectively by understanding potential side effects and interactions. Remember, a little knowledge goes a long way in ensuring your herbal journey is healthy.

The Dose Conundrum: How Much Is Enough?

Earlier in this chapter, I mentioned the importance of figuring out the dosage dilemma. Finding out the right amount of herbs to take can be tricky. Since there aren't clear guidelines, it often becomes a guessing game.

- **Lack of standards:** Unlike your grandma's cookie recipe, herbal dosages aren't standardized. This means it's hard to know how much you need to take to feel the benefits without overdoing it.

- **Finding the balance:** Start with small doses and see how your body reacts. It's like taste testing a new dish—starting with a small bite is better!

Stories of Misconceptions

- **Herbs as cure-alls:** Some people think herbs can fix everything overnight. Sorry, but herbs aren't magic wands. They need some time and patience to work their charm.

- **Unregulated formulations:** Herbal products can vary in quality. It's like buying a mystery box—you don't always know what you're getting. Stick to reputable brands to avoid surprises.

Embracing Herbal Medicine Responsibly

Understanding the limits of herbal remedies helps you use them wisely. They have great potential, but they also come with constraints. In the following sections, we'll explore specific herbs, how to use them, and tips for adding them to your wellness routine safely and effectively.

Approach herbal medicine with open eyes and a small amount of caution. It's a journey, not a sprint; with the proper knowledge, you can enjoy the benefits while staying safe. So, grab your tea, sit back, and let's explore the world of herbs together!

Myth Versus Fact Quiz

Now that we've explored the common myths and facts surrounding herbal remedies, it's time to put your knowledge to the test. Take the quiz, uncover the truths, and challenge any lingering myths you might have about herbal remedies. Remember, knowledge is the key to making informed decisions about your well-being. Happy myth-busting!

Instructions: True or False

1. Herbal medicine is always supported by robust scientific research.

    a. True

    b. False

2. Taking herbal medicine without informing your healthcare provider about other medications you're on is safe.

    a. True

    b. False

3. Herbal remedies are natural, so they are always safe.

    a. True

    b. False

4. The benefits of herbal medicine are not always evident after a single dose.

    a. True

    b. False

5. Herbal medicine is a cheaper alternative to conventional medications.

    a. True

    b. False

6. Herbal medicine and homeopathy are the same thing.

    a. True

    b. False

7. You can positively identify plants for herbal use without expert guidance.

    a. True

    b. False

8. Combining herbal therapy with prescription medications increases the potential for interactions and side effects.

    a. True

    b. False

9. The dose of herbs required for the claimed effect is well-established.

    a. True

    b. False

10. Herbal remedies are cure-alls, providing immediate and miraculous results.

    a. True

    b. False

Scoring

8–10 correct: Herbal myth buster! You've got a solid grasp of the realities of herbal medicine.

5–7 correct: Informed explorer. You're on the right track, but there's always more to learn.

0–4 correct: Myth enthusiast. Time to brush up on your herbal knowledge; this quiz is a great place to start!

Answers

1. False
2. False
3. False
4. True
5. True
6. False
7. False
8. True
9. False
10. False

Reality Check Complete: Myth-Busting Herbal Remedies

We've busted the myths and cleared up the confusion around herbal remedies. Here's what we've learned:

- **No one-size-fits-all:** Herbal medicine isn't a magic cure for everything. It has its limits, and what works for one person might not work for another.

- **Keep it real:** Having realistic expectations about what herbs can and can't do is essential.

- **Safety first:** Always consult healthcare professionals before using herbal treatments to ensure their safety.

Moving Forward

Now that you have a clearer understanding of herbal medicine, it's time to put this knowledge to use. As you start exploring herbs for your health routine, remember to make informed decisions and keep your healthcare provider in the loop.

Next Chapter: The Art of Identifying Herbs

Our next adventure awaits as we leave behind the myths and step into the light of truth. We'll learn how to identify herbs and understand the importance of ethical harvesting. Knowing which herbs you're using and where they come from is as important as knowing how to use them.

Let's dive into the fascinating world of herb identification. We'll uncover the secrets hidden in each leaf and stem, helping you make the most of nature's gifts.

Chapter 4

BOTANICAL MASTER

Imagine you're in a garden full of plants that can help you feel better and nurture your body. In this chapter, I will show you how to be a plant detective and spot these helpful plants in this vast world we're still exploring. Let's get started!

Basics of Identifying Medicinal Plants

Step 1: Observe the Plant's Environment

Look around where the plant is growing. Is it hot or cold? Is it sunny or shady? Some plants only grow in certain climates and places, so knowing this can help you identify them.

Step 2: Examine the Stems and Branches

Check out the plant's stems and branches. Are they thick or thin, smooth or bumpy, green or brown? The look and feel of the stems and branches can give you important clues.

Step 3: Inspect the Leaves

Look at the leaves closely. Are they big or small? What shape are they? How are they arranged on the stem? Are they opposite each other, taking turns, or in circles? This is very important for identifying the plant.

Step 4: Look at the Flowers

If the plant has flowers, take a good look at them. What color are they? What shape are they? How are the flowers arranged? Consider flowers as a plant's ID card.

Step 5: Check for Fruits and Seeds

If the plant has fruits or seeds, these can also help you determine what plant it is. Look at their size, shape, and color.

Step 6: Use a Field Guide or Dichotomous Key

A field guide is a book with pictures and descriptions of plants. A dichotomous key asks questions about the plant's features to help you identify it. Using these tools can make plant identification much easier, and later in this chapter, we'll explore this tool in depth. Nevertheless, always look at multiple features of the plant, not just one.

Step 7: Consider the Plant's Organoleptic Characteristics

This means using your senses: color, taste, feel, and smell of the plant. These can be useful for confirming the plant's identity. Just be careful and make sure the plant is safe before tasting.

Step 8: Understand the Plant's Medicinal Properties

Knowing what the plant is used for can also help you identify it. For example:

- Chamomile is often used for anxiety and relaxation.

- Echinacea treats or prevents colds, flu, and infections.

- Ginkgo's leaf extract treats conditions like asthma, bronchitis, fatigue, and tinnitus.

We can't let Sherlock Holmes have all the fun, especially when being a plant detective, which, in this case, is fascinating and valuable. Using guides, you can identify many plants by looking at the environment, stems, leaves, flowers, fruits, and seeds. Remember to be careful and respectful of nature. Enjoy your journey into the world of medicinal plants.

Mastering Medicinal Plant Identification

Ready to level up your plant detective game? In this part of the chapter, we'll dive into advanced ways to spot those magical medicinal plants. Get ready to explore field guides, mobile apps, and other cool tools to become a pro at identifying these green wonders.

Advanced Technique 1: Using Field Guides

What's a Field Guide?

Think of a field guide as a plant encyclopedia you can carry around. It's packed with pictures and descriptions of plants.

How to Use a Field Guide:

- **Look up the plant:** Spot a plant that catches your eye. Flip through the guide to find a matching picture.

- **Compare features:** Check the plant's leaves, stems, flowers, and fruits against the guide. Make sure they match. Some plants are very similar but have incredibly different effects, including being poisonous.

- **Read the description:** Dive into the guide's description to learn more about the plant, including its medicinal uses.

Pro tip: Field guides often have a glossary for tricky terms. Don't hesitate to look things up—it's not cheating!

Advanced Technique 2: Using Mobile Apps

What's a Plant Identification App?

A mobile app is like having a plant expert in your pocket. Using technology is beneficial, especially with apps like PlantSnap, PictureThis, and iNaturalist, which help you identify plants using your smartphone.

How to Use a Mobile App:

- **Take a photo:** Open the app and snap a clear picture of the plant.

- **Analyze the photo:** The app will analyze the photo and suggest possible matches.

- **Compare results:** Look at the app's suggestions and compare them to your plant. Check multiple features to confirm the ID.

- **Read more:** Most apps provide info about the plant's uses, including medicinal properties.

Pro tip: Make sure your photos are well-lit and focused. Blurry photos confuse the app and might make it think your daisy is a dandelion.

Advanced Technique 3: Using Dichotomous Keys

What's a Dichotomous Key?

A dichotomous key is like a choose-your-own-adventure book for plants. It helps you identify plants by asking a series of questions.

How to Use a Dichotomous Key:

- **Start with the first question:** Answer the first question about a plant's feature, like, "Are the leaves needle-like or broad?"

- **Follow the path:** Each answer leads you to the next question. Keep answering until you reach the plant's identity.

- **Double-check:** Look at the plant's other features once you have a name.

Pro tip: Dichotomous keys can be tricky. Practice with common plants to get the hang of it.

Advanced Technique 4: Using Organoleptic Characteristics

What are Organoleptic Characteristics?

You can sense these traits, like taste, smell, color, and texture.

How to Use Organoleptic Characteristics:

- **Observe:** Look at the plant's color and texture.

- **Smell:** Gently sniff the plant. Some have distinct scents.

- **Taste:** *Only* taste if you're confident the plant is safe. Taste can help confirm its identity.

Pro tip: Always be cautious when tasting plants. Some can be harmful if misidentified—you don't want to mistake a delicious mint for a nasty nettle!

Advanced Technique 5: DNA Barcoding Made Simple

What Is DNA Barcoding?

It's identifying species using short, standardized DNA sequences.

Why Use DNA Barcoding?

It provides accurate and reliable identification of plants.

How Effective Is It?

Scientific studies show it works well for distinguishing different plant species. For example, research published in the *Plant Biotechnology Journal* by Mishra et al. in 2015 supports its effectiveness.

Pro tip: Always ensure you use a well-preserved sample for DNA barcoding to get the most accurate results.

Advanced Technique 6: Remote Sensing Techniques Simplified

What Is It?

It's using tools like satellite imagery and drones to study vegetation and identify plants from a distance.

Why Use It?

It provides valuable insights into plant patterns across large areas.

Pro tip: Check the resolution of the imagery for better accuracy.

Advanced Technique 7: Machine Learning and Artificial Intelligence Made Easy

What Are They?

It's using computers to learn and recognize patterns in plant features.

Why Use Them?

It helps identify plants more accurately and quickly.

Pro tip: Train your AI model with diverse plant data for better results.

Becoming a master plant detective takes practice and the right tools. Field guides, mobile apps, dichotomous keys, and your senses are all valuable in identifying medicinal plants. Keep exploring, learning, and enjoying the wonderful world of plants.

Ethical Harvesting: Harvesting the Right Way

Learning how to gather your herbal treasures without leaving any destruction behind is important. As much as the world of herbs is there to give, it's our duty not to take that for granted. They say, "Hell hath no fury like a woman scorned," and I'd like to think Mother Nature wouldn't hesitate to reprimand us should we abuse her natural world. So together, we're going to learn ethical and sustainable harvesting practices that'll leave nature as beautiful as we found it.

What Is Ethical Harvesting?

Ethical harvesting means collecting herbs in a way that's kind to the plants and the environment. It's like being a considerate guest at nature's party.

Learn to Identify

First things first: Know your plants! Accurate identification is critical to ethical wildcrafting. You don't want to mistake a helpful herb for a harmful one. So become a plant detective and learn everything you can about your leafy friends.

Eat Your Weeds

Start with the common stuff! Harvest those abundant, resilient plants (aka "weeds") that are everywhere. This way, you won't accidentally overpick the rare ones. Think of it as starting with the junk food of the plant world before moving on to the gourmet.

Protect Vulnerable Plant Populations

Be extra careful with endangered or rare plants. Get familiar with watch lists from groups like United Plant Savers. If a plant is on the list, give it a pass and let it thrive.

Follow Local Guidelines:

Some places have rules about picking plants. Know the guidelines and follow them.

Avoid Overharvesting

Don't be a plant hog! Only take what you need, and leave plenty behind. This helps plants regenerate and keeps their populations healthy. Remember, sharing is caring—even with plants. In addition, make it a habit to rotate the harvesting area; don't keep picking from the same spot. Give areas time to recover by rotating where you harvest.

Bring Proper Tools

Use the right tools to avoid damaging plants. Sharp scissors, pruning shears, or special harvesting knives are your friends here. Think of it as giving the plant a nice haircut instead of a bad trim.

Harvest in the Right Season

Pick plants when they're most abundant, usually in the growing season. Avoid harvesting when plants are stressed.

Be Opportunistic (in a Good Way)

Grab the chance to harvest ethically. Consider how abundant the plant is, what you need, and how the ecosystem can bounce back. It's like shopping during a sale—take advantage, but don't go overboard.

Assess Your Environment

Check out the area before you harvest. Stay away from polluted spots like industrial sites or busy roads. You wouldn't want to eat herbs soaked in car fumes.

Be Undetectable

Leave no trace. Tread lightly, avoid trampling the surrounding plants, and make it look like you were never there. Think of yourself as an herbal ninja.

Offer Gratitude to the Sacred Plants

Show some love to the plants. Acknowledge their role in your well-being and express your appreciation. A little gratitude goes a long way.

Embrace Ethical Harvesting

By following these principles, you're not just preserving plant populations; you're also keeping the ecosystem healthy. Here's a handy five-step guide for responsible wildcrafting:

- **Be super careful:** Leave the environment better than you found it.

- **Know the plants:** Avoid harvesting rare and endangered species.

- **Know the land:** Choose healthy landscapes, avoiding polluted areas.

- **Know the rules:** Follow legal guidelines and get any necessary permits.

- **Take a little:** Harvest conservatively—no more than 10% of what you find.

By incorporating these practices into your wildcrafting adventures, you help ensure the longevity of medicinal plants and their ecosystems. Remember, ethical harvesting isn't just a responsibility; it's a joyful dance with nature.

Best Practices in Preservation and Storage of Herbs

You've harvested your herbs responsibly—great job! Now, let's make sure they stay fresh and potent. Preserving and storing herbs properly is essential. Follow these simple steps to keep your herbal treasures in top shape.

Dehydrating Herbs

Use a Dehydrator

Set the dehydrator temperature between 95 °F and 110 °F. This low-and-slow method preserves the herbs without reducing their medicinal kick.

Air-Drying

For a natural, electricity-free option, air-dry your herbs. Keep them out of direct sunlight and ensure good airflow to prevent mold. It takes longer but works like a charm!

Oven Drying

If you're using an oven, keep the temperature low, around 100 °F. Many ovens have dehydrator settings, making this a convenient option without needing extra gadgets.

Freeze-Drying Herbs

Freeze drying is the gold standard for preserving herbs. It keeps vitamins, minerals, antioxidants, and essential oils intact, maintaining the herb's flavor, aroma, color, and texture. Properly stored, freeze-dried herbs can last for years.

Tincturing Herbs

What's Tincturing?

Tincturing involves preserving herbs in high-proof alcohol, which extracts their medicinal properties. This method creates a potent herbal remedy that can be stored for years.

How to Tincture:

- **Extraction process:** Soak herbs in alcohol to extract their medicinal goodies.
- **Storage:** Because of the alcohol, tinctures last long, perfect for your herbal medicine cabinet.

Old-Fashioned Preservation Methods

Hang Drying

Tie bundles of herbs and hang them upside down in a cool, dry place. This method is simple, effective, and doesn't need electricity.

Preserving herbs can be fun and easy! Proper storage ensures your herbs stay potent and effective whether you choose dehydration, freeze-drying, tincturing, or hang drying. Remember these tips, and your herbal treasures will be good to go for a long time.

Turning Over a New Leaf

Let's recap some key takeaways from this chapter:

- **Identifying medicinal plants:** Use multiple methods, such as observing the environment and examining stems, leaves, flowers, and fruits. Utilize field guides, dichotomous keys, organoleptic characteristics, and more for accurate identification.

- **Advanced techniques:** Incorporate tools like field guides and mobile apps to become a plant ID pro.

- **Ethical harvesting practices:** Follow principles of ethical wildcrafting—protect vulnerable plants, avoid overharvesting, and show gratitude.

- **Preservation and storage:** Master the art of preserving and storing herbs using dehydration, freeze-drying, and tincturing to keep them potent.

Next Chapter: Awareness and Safety

As we turn over a new leaf, prepare for the next chapter on herbal interactions. Safety is vital, and understanding how herbs interact with each other is crucial. Join us to explore the nuances of herbal interactions, ensuring your herbal journey is enriching and safe.

Chapter 5

AWARENESS AND SAFETY

Did you know that even nature's gifts have instructions for safe use? Safety is paramount in the intricate world of herbal remedies. This chapter will discuss ways to ensure your well-being isn't at risk in the herbal world and that the path to natural health is secure and effective. The more we learn and understand the herbal world, the more important it is to know how to use or incorporate them into our daily routine.

Now, let me tell a little story. Back when I was young, my parents used to force me to take conventional medication when I was sick. I hated taking them—and I still do—due to how they tasted and sounded like some alien language. However, after being diagnosed with a chronic illness, I was in desperate need of finding a safer, effective, and more natural way to take care of my health. So, I rolled up my sleeves, did some research, and learned all about how drugs, herbs, and our bodies can coexist in harmony. Now, I'm here to pass that knowledge on to you!

By the time you finish this chapter, you'll be strutting around like a pro, confidently using herbs, deciphering tricky interactions with medications, sticking to dosing guidelines like a boss, and spotting quality herbs from a mile away—just like you can sniff out a fake designer handbag!

So, let's embark on this wild adventure together. We'll unravel the mysteries of herbal safety and arm you with all the tools you need to tap into the amazing benefits of nature's medicine cabinet without breaking a sweat.

Understanding Interactions with Medications and Health Conditions

Natural remedies are the shining stars in the wonderful world of holistic health. Herbs have been our trusty side-kicks for thousands of years, helping us fight off ailments, boost our energy, and improve our overall health. However, before you dive headfirst into the herb garden, you should know that herbs can sometimes mess with your medications. Understanding these interactions is crucial, especially if you take prescribed meds.

The Herb–Drug Dance

Herbs, like medications, contain active ingredients that can significantly affect your body. When these herbal compounds interact with the meds you're taking, they can change how your medications work, cause side effects, or even lead to serious health issues. There are two main interactions to watch out for: pharmacokinetic and pharmacodynamic.

Pharmacokinetic interactions are about how your body handles drugs—how they're absorbed, distributed, metabolized, and excreted. Herbs can change these processes, affecting the amount of medication in your bloodstream. Take St. John's wort, for example. This popular herb for depression can speed up the liver's metabolism of certain drugs, like antidepressants, making them less effective.

Pharmacodynamic interactions are about the combined effects of herbs and drugs on your body. For instance, ginkgo, a go-to for improving brain function, can prevent blood from clotting. If you're also taking blood thinners like warfarin or aspirin, this combo can increase your risk of bleeding.

It's safe to say that herbs are like nature's little powerhouses; they can mess with how your body works, just like medications do. When herbs and drugs get together, they can have a bit of a turf war, changing how well each one works and how safe they are. The NCCIH has some great info on this. They remind us that even though herbs are natural, they can act just like regular meds in your body. Moreover, since the strength of herbs can vary, mixing them with medications might lead to some unexpected shenanigans.

Let's look at some common herbs, their key ingredients, and how they might team up with or fight against different drugs.

Herb-Drug Interactions: The Fun, the Fussy, and the Facts

I often like to think of herbs as the sassy cousins of medications—they can be helpful, but sometimes, they don't play well together. Let's break down some common herbs and how they might shake things up with your meds.

The Usual Suspects

Black Cohosh (Actaea racemosa)

- What it does: It may make drugs like amiodarone, fexofenadine, glyburide, and many statins less effective.

- Fun fact: It's like that friend who always turns the volume down at a party—sometimes, you want them to let things be!

Curcumin (Curcuma longa)

- What it does: It boosts sulfasalazine levels but can lower the levels of many antidepressants and antipsychotics.

- Fun fact: Think of it as the overenthusiastic friend who lifts some people but brings others down.

Echinacea

- What it does: It can affect enzymes (CYP1A2 and CYP3A4) that process antipsychotic and antidepressant drugs.

- Fun fact: It's like that overzealous cheerleader—great for the immune system but can be too much for some meds.

Garlic (Allium sativum)

- What it does: It lowers concentrations of drugs like colchicine, digoxin, and verapamil. Its blood-thinning properties can also be tricky during surgery.

- Fun fact: Garlic's the life of the cardiovascular party but sometimes causes chaos, especially when sharp objects (like scalpels) are involved.

Ginkgo (Ginkgo biloba)

- What it does: It prevents blood from clotting, increasing bleeding risk when combined with blood thinners.

- Fun fact: It's the ultimate peacekeeper in the brain department, but watch out when it meets blood thinners—it just can't stop itself from getting too friendly.

Ginseng (American and Asian)

- What it does: American ginseng lowers the international normalized ratio (INR) in patients on warfarin, while Asian ginseng can reduce the effectiveness of various drugs.
- Fun fact: It's like the sibling who wants to help but sometimes creates more work for everyone.

Goldenseal (Hydrastis canadensis)

- What it does: It inhibits enzymes that metabolize many drugs, making it a bad idea to mix with most meds.
- Fun fact: Goldenseal is the stubborn one who likes things their way and doesn't mix well with others.

Green Tea (Camellia sinensis)

- What it does: It increases simvastatin levels and may interfere with other medications.
- Fun fact: It's the trendy health nut that sometimes overdoes it with antioxidants, causing serious uncertainty in other meds.

Kava Kava (Piper methysticum)

- What it does: It interferes with the metabolism of many drugs, particularly those used during surgery or with central nervous system depressants.
- Fun fact: Kava Kava is that laid-back beach bum who sometimes doesn't know when to stop chilling out.

Milk Thistle (Silybum marianum)

- What it does: It reduces the metabolism of drugs like losartan, warfarin, and diazepam.

- Fun fact: It's the detox friend who sometimes forgets that not everyone needs to detox as much as they do.

St. John's Wort (Hypericum perforatum)

- What it does: It interacts with many medications, reducing their effectiveness.

- Fun fact: It's the overachiever who thinks they can handle anything but ends up causing a mess.

Your Balanced Approach to Wellness

You want your medication or herbal remedy like Goldilocks's porridge—not too much or too little, but just right. Taking too much can lead to unwanted side effects or even make your treatment less effective. On the flip side, not taking enough means you might not get the full benefits.

Stick to the Recipe: Recommended Doses

Think of sticking to recommended doses like following a recipe—it's the secret sauce to getting the best results without any kitchen disasters. Trust me, more isn't always better, and sticking to the plan keeps you on the path to feeling your best. So, please resist the urge to sprinkle extra herbs, thinking it'll improve everything. Too much of a good thing can lead to some not-so-fun side effects!

Team Up with Your Health Squad

Your health journey must involve walking hand in hand with your healthcare providers. They have the know-how to tailor your plan just for you, especially if you're a seasoned pro or managing a few health hiccups. So don't forget to call the experts before adding herbal remedies to your routine.

Crack the Herbal Code: Research Challenges

Now, let's talk about the wild world of herbal research. It's like trying to find a needle in a haystack, with only a few herbs getting the full spotlight. Understanding these studies is like deciphering a secret code—there's a lot of debate and confusion swirling around. But hey, even negative studies have their silver lining, helping us separate fact from fiction. Just like in Chinese medicine, your herbal journey might have ups and downs, but that's all part of the adventure!

So, my herbal enthusiasts, let's embrace these principles and let your confidence be your guide. With a small amount of know-how and a dash of determination, you'll be rocking the herbal scene like a pro. Your journey to natural health is all about you, and armed with these tips, you've got everything you need to navigate it like a champ!

Keeping It Safe and Sound: Why Doses Matter

Remember, when it comes to doses, it's all about finding that sweet spot where you get the most benefit with the fewest side effects. Stay on track with your doses, and you'll be on your way to feeling your best in no time!

Dosage Guidelines by Age

Here's a quick guide to help you hit the right notes (*Dosing Guidelines*, n.d.):

- 1 month old: 1/18–1/14 of the adult dose
- 1–6 months old: 1/14–1/7 of the adult dose
- 6–12 months old: 1/7–1/5 of the adult dose
- 1–2 years old: 1/5–1/4 of the adult dose

- 2–4 years old: 1/4–1/3 of the adult dose
- 4–6 years old: 1/3–2/5 of the adult dose
- 6–9 years old: 2/5–1/2 of the adult dose
- 9–14 years old: 1/2–2/3 of the adult dose
- 14–18 years old: 2/3 to full adult dose
- 18–60 years old: 1 full adult dose
- 60 years old and over: 3/4 of the adult dose or less

The Bottom Line

Herbs can be great, but they can also be like unruly party guests when mixed with medications. Ensure you know how they interact, stick to the proper doses, and always check with your healthcare provider to keep everything in harmony.

Assessing Quality and Purity in Herbs

Embarking on your herbal journey comes with a responsibility—ensuring the quality and purity of your chosen herbal products.

Investigating Herb Makers: Sherlock Style

Before you grab any herbal product off the shelf, let's play detective and snoop around the manufacturer's background. Consider it as checking out a new restaurant—you want to ensure they're not serving soggy fries. Check out reviews, testimonials, and anything else you can dig up about the company. A solid reputation is your best bet for quality herbs.

Mind the Herbal Highway: Avoiding Traffic Jams

Just like you wouldn't hitch a ride with a driver who's had too much coffee, be wary of herbs sneaking into the country through dodgy channels. Stick to the ones that have passed through official checkpoints—they're like the herbs with a stamped passport, ready to party safely in your system.

Natural Doesn't Mean Safe: Beware the Charm of "Natural"

Sure, herbs are all-natural, but that doesn't mean they're all as harmless as a bunny rabbit. Some can be pretty unsafe and leave some damage. Stick to recommended doses and give the side-eye to any products making wild claims. Authenticity and transparency should be your best friends in this herb-filled adventure.

The Herbal Authenticity Test: Sniffing Out the Real Deal

As mentioned previously, authenticity is critical when picking herbal products. Think of it as choosing a genuine Picasso over a cheap knockoff. Dive deep into the manufacturer's safety and quality control measures. A commitment to these aspects means you're getting the good stuff that'll actually do what it promises.

Peeking Behind the Herbal Curtain: Unveiling the Magic

Lastly, let's peek behind the scenes of the herbal manufacturing process. Think of it as glancing into the kitchen of your favorite restaurant; again, transparency is a must here. So, make sure the manufacturer isn't hiding any secrets. A commitment to quality means every batch of herbs meets the highest standards.

Herb-tastic Takeaways

We've discussed a lot in our herbal adventure, but remember these key takeaways:

- **Investigate herb makers:** Check out those behind the curtain to make sure they're not just blowing smoke.

- **Mind the herbal highway:** Stick to the official routes to avoid sketchy herbs.

- **Natural isn't always nice:** Just because it's natural doesn't mean it's all sunshine and rainbows.

- **Authenticity matters:** Choose the real deal over cheap imitations.

- **Transparency is key:** Make sure the manufacturing process is as clear as a sunny day.

You're ready to take on the herbal world like a boss, armed with your newfound herbal wisdom and a sprinkle of humor. Go forth, brave herbal adventurer, and may your journey be filled with laughter, joy, and the best darn herbs you've ever tasted!

Herbal Safety Fun Checkup

Ready to dive into the herbal world with confidence and a sprinkle of fun? We've got just the thing for you: our herbal safety checklist, your trusty sidekick for ensuring your herbal journey is smooth sailing.

Interactions Adventure: Are You Prepared?

- Have you checked if any herbs you're taking might have a tango with your current meds?

- Do you know how certain herbs might shake hands with specific health conditions?

Dosing Dilemma: Are You on Track?

- Do you stick to the recommended doses for your herbs like glue?

- Are you clued up on dosing guidelines tailored to your age group, especially if you're a seasoned senior?

Quality Quest: Sniffing Out the Good Stuff

- Do you background check the herb maker before hitting that "buy" button?

- Are you wary of herbs sneaking into the country through backdoors? We're talking about official checkpoints only!

- Have you given a side-eye to the authenticity and safety measures of the herb maker?

Health Hero Collaboration: Team Up for Success

- Do you chat with your doctor before adding herbal goodies to your wellness routine?

- If you're a wise old owl or have health quirks, do you devise a personalized plan with your doctor?

Reflecting on Herbal Adventures: A Think Tank Session

- Are you aware of the challenges in herbal research, like how only a few herbs get their moment in the research spotlight?

- Do you approach your herbal experiences with a mix of Sherlock Holmes's smarts and Mary Poppins's optimism?

Wrapping Up

As we wrap up this chapter of our herb adventure, here's the lowdown:

- **Understanding interactions:** Know how herbs and meds interact for a smooth sailing journey.

- **Dosing guidelines:** Stick to the recommended doses like a boss to avoid herb-related adventures.

- **Quality quest:** Sniff out the good stuff and avoid shady herb deals.

- **Health hero collaboration:** Team up with your doctor for a tailor-made herb plan for you.

Armed with your herbal wisdom, you're ready to take on the herbal world like a pro. So go forth, adventurous herb explorer, and may your journey be filled with laughter, joy, and the best herbs you've ever tasted!

Chapter 6

LEARNING TO PREPARE

Picture yourself as a kitchen wizard, brewing magical potions from ordinary herbs. This chapter is like your very own Hogwarts, but instead of wands and spells, you'll be wielding mortar and pestle, stirring up the healing magic of nature. Our mission? To teach you the tricks of the trade in herbal preparation. By the time you finish this chapter, you'll be a master potion maker, whipping up remedies that suit your needs like a boss. So, grab your cauldron, and let's get brewing!

Exploring Diverse Forms of Herbal Remedies

Let's embark on an adventure through the world of herbal remedies! We have many incredible ways to tap into nature's power and boost our health.

First, let's chat about teas. They're the official starting point of herbal remedies. Just steep some herbs in hot water, and bam, you've got yourself a comforting and tasty brew. Herbal teas are like nature's little magic potions, packed with all sorts of goodness to boost your health and mood. I frequently use herbal teas because they make it easier to use herbs, whether dry or fresh.

As the chapter unfolds, we'll dive into the world of herbal teas and uncover their excellent benefits, along with some

69

fun facts to spice things up! Whether you're into calming chamomile or spicy ginger, there's a tea for everyone.

Now, onto salves. These are like herbal ointments that you can rub on your skin. They're fantastic for soothing achy muscles, moisturizing dry skin, or even healing minor cuts and scrapes. Plus, they're portable, so you can carry your herbal remedy anywhere.

Moving right along, we've got tinctures. These bad boys are super-concentrated herbal extracts that you can take drop by drop. They're like the turbocharged version of herbs, packing a serious punch in a tiny amount.

Finally, we've got capsules. These are like little herbal pills that you can swallow with water. They're perfect if you're not a fan of the taste of herbs or if you're looking for a convenient way to get your daily dose of herbal goodness.

Now that we've covered the basics let's dive deeper into the world of herbal remedies. Each type offers its own set of benefits and uses, making it easy to find the perfect herbal remedy for your needs. Whether you're sipping on a cup of tea, applying a soothing salve, or swallowing a capsule, you're sure to find a way to harness nature's healing powers and boost your well-being.

Expanding the discussion to specific herbal teas, these infusions offer delightful flavors and unique health benefits.

Chamomile Tea

- Benefits: Known for its calming properties, chamomile tea is perfect for winding down after a long day. It can help with anxiety, insomnia, and even digestive issues.

- Fun fact: Did you know that chamomile tea has been used for centuries as a natural remedy for everything, from colds to menstrual cramps? Plus, it smells fantastic!

Peppermint Tea

- Benefits: Peppermint tea is like a breath of fresh air for your digestive system. It can soothe upset stomachs, ease indigestion, and even relieve headaches.

- Fun fact: Peppermint tea isn't just delicious; it's also great for keeping pesky bugs away! Insects hate the smell of peppermint, so sipping on some tea can help keep them at bay.

Ginger Tea

- Benefits: Ginger tea is a powerhouse for fighting inflammation and boosting your immune system. It can also help with nausea, motion sickness, and sore throats.

- Fun fact: Ginger tea has been used for centuries in traditional medicine to treat various ailments, from arthritis to the common cold. Plus, it adds a spicy kick to your tea!

Lemon Balm Tea

- Benefits: Lemon balm tea is like a ray of sunshine in a cup. It can help improve mood, reduce stress, and promote relaxation. Plus, it's great for digestion and can even help with sleep.

- Fun fact: Lemon balm tea is often used in aromatherapy to uplift the spirits and boost energy levels. Just the smell of it can put a smile on your face!

Hibiscus Tea

- Benefits: Hibiscus tea is bursting with antioxidants, making it great for heart health. It can help lower blood pressure, reduce cholesterol levels, and even aid in weight loss.

- Fun fact: Hibiscus tea isn't just good for you; it's also beautiful! The vibrant red color comes from the petals of the hibiscus flower, which are rich in anthocyanins.

So there you have it, a delightful lineup of herbal teas and their amazing benefits. Whether you're looking to relax, refresh, or revitalize, there's tea out there for everyone. So brew yourself a cup and enjoy all the goodness nature offers!

Crafting Herbal Remedies with Confidence

As you embark on your journey into the world of herbal remedies, you must equip yourself with the knowledge and skills needed to prepare these natural concoctions effectively. In this chapter, we'll delve into the best practices and common mistakes to avoid when crafting herbal remedies, ensuring you can do so confidently and succeed.

Best Practices

- **Choosing high-quality ingredients:** The quality of your herbs and other ingredients will significantly impact the potency and effectiveness of your herbal remedies. Always opt for organic, sustainably sourced herbs to ensure purity and efficacy.

- **Following proper dosage guidelines:** Herbal remedies can be potent, so although I've mentioned it before, it's crucial to adhere to the recommended dosage guidelines. Overconsumption can lead to adverse effects, so measure your ingredients carefully and follow instructions closely.

- **Using the right preparation method:** Different herbs require different preparation methods to extract their beneficial properties effectively. Whether you're making tea, tincture, salve, or capsule, research the appropriate method for your specific herb to maximize its potency.

- **Maintaining proper hygiene:** Just like cooking in the kitchen, cleanliness is essential when crafting herbal remedies. Wash your hands thoroughly, sanitize your equipment, and work in a clean, clutter-free environment to prevent contamination and ensure the purity of your remedies.

- **Labeling and dating your creations:** Proper labeling is vital to staying organized and ensuring the safety of your herbal remedies. Clearly label each remedy with its name, ingredients, preparation date, and expiration date (if applicable) to avoid confusion and prevent the use of expired products.

Common Mistakes to Avoid

- **Using incorrect herbs:** Not all herbs suit every individual or health condition. Avoid using herbs without proper research or consultation, as they may interact with medications or exacerbate existing health issues.

- **Ignoring safety precautions:** Some herbs can be toxic in large doses or misused. Always research the safety precautions associated with each herb, and consult with a healthcare professional if you have any concerns or underlying health conditions.

- **Overlooking allergic reactions:** Allergies to herbs are not uncommon, so it's essential to be vigilant and monitor for any adverse reactions when trying new remedies. Start with small doses and observe how your body reacts before increasing the dosage or frequency of use.

- **Storing remedies improperly:** Proper storage is crucial for maintaining your herbal remedies' potency and shelf life. Store them in a cool, dark place away from direct sunlight and moisture, and avoid storing them near heat sources or in humid environments.

- **Neglecting to keep records:** Recording your herbal remedies, including the ingredients used, preparation methods, and dosage regimens, is essential for future reference and troubleshooting. Maintain a detailed journal or logbook to document your experiences and track your progress.

By following these best practices and avoiding common mistakes, you'll be well-equipped to craft herbal remedies confidently and precisely, harnessing nature's power to support your health and well-being.

In-Depth Guidance on Preparation Methods

Embarking on the journey of herbal preparation involves understanding the types of remedies and mastering the art of crafting them. Here's an in-depth guide on preparing various herbal remedies:

Herbal Salves: Soothing Nature's Touch

Make Herb-Infused Oil

- Craft herb-infused oils using dried herbs for better preservation.
- Opt for dried herbs to prevent spoilage from moisture.

Make Your Salve

Ingredients:

> 1-ounce beeswax (or carnauba wax for a vegan option), bar or granules
>
> 4 ounces herb-infused oils of your choice (pick one or mix them up)
>
> 10–20 drops of essential oil of your choice (optional)

Directions:

1. If using a bar of beeswax, first wrap it in an old towel and break it into small chunks using a hammer.
2. Melt the beeswax in a double boiler over low heat.
3. Stir in herbal oils until mixed well.
4. Remove from heat, add essential oils, and pour into containers.
5. Let it cool completely before storing it in a cool place for 1–3 years.

How to Make Herbal Tinctures

1. Choose herbs with medicinal properties, ensuring they're safe for your health.
2. Fill a mason jar 1/3 full with chopped herbs.

3. Pour alcohol over the herbs, covering them completely and leaving 2 inches of alcohol above.

4. Seal the jar tightly, shake it, and label it with the herb name, alcohol type, and date.

5. Place the jar in a warm, dark place, shaking it daily for 4–6 weeks.

6. Stain the herbs and transfer the tincture to labeled glass dropper bottles after steeping.

Remember, each step in your herbal preparation journey is like a dance with nature. Follow these guidelines, avoid common mistakes, and soon, you'll craft herbal remedies like a pro.

Personalizing Herbal Remedies for Specific Needs

Ensuring you have herbal remedies that meet your needs, especially as you age, is essential. In this part of the chapter, we will discuss how to make herbal remedies that suit seniors with quirks and sensitivities. We'll dive into the intricacies of tailoring herbal treatments for seniors, empowering them to take control of their well-being and vitality.

Step 1: Understanding Seniors' Health Needs

Assessing Health Challenges

- Identify common health issues affecting seniors, such as arthritis, insomnia, digestive problems, and cognitive decline.

- Recognize the importance of addressing these concerns with gentle yet effective herbal remedies.

Consulting Reputable Sources

- Refer to trusted books, websites, and experts specializing in herbal medicine for seniors.

- Consider resources focusing on evidence-based information and safety considerations for older adults.

Step 2: Tailoring Herbal Remedies for Seniors

Choosing Appropriate Herbs

- Select herbs known for their efficacy and safety in addressing seniors' health concerns.

- Prioritize gentle herbs with anti-inflammatory, sedative, digestive, and cognitive-supportive properties.

Considering Sensitivities and Interactions

- Consider seniors' potential sensitivities, allergies, and medication interactions.

- Opt for herbs with minimal side effects and low risk of adverse reactions.

Customizing Dosages and Formulations

- Adjust herbal dosages based on seniors' age, weight, and overall health status.

- Explore different forms of herbal preparations, such as teas, tinctures, capsules, and topical applications.

Step 3: Power Up the Potency

Boosting the Right Strength

Seniors might need a little extra oomph in their herbal mix. Pick herbs that pack a punch, but treat them with kindness.

Go-To Sources for Strength

Look for trusty guides that spill the beans on how strong those herbs should be for our seniors. We don't want them bouncing off the walls!

Step 4: Sensitivity Smarts

Handle With Care

Some seniors might be as delicate as a flower when it comes to certain herbs. Take it easy and start slowly to avoid any surprises.

Testing the Waters

Start with a sprinkle, not a downpour. Slowly ramp up the herb power while watching for any funny business.

Step 5: Calling in the Pros

Doctor Knows Best

It's always good to chat with the doctor before diving into the herbal world, especially if you're already juggling meds or health issues.

Expert Advice

Let the pros work their magic. Healthcare providers can sprinkle some personalized guidance on your herbal concoctions.

Tailoring herbal remedies to seniors' health concerns requires careful consideration and expertise. By understanding their unique needs and preferences and harnessing the power of herbal medicine, they can enjoy enhanced well-being and vitality in their golden years.

Resources for Further Exploration

- **JAMA:** To get the lowdown on herbs for both body and mind

- **Cancer Research UK:** To find herbal help for those facing cancer

- **Royal College of Psychiatrists:** To look into the herbal helpers for mental health

- **PubMed:** To discover herbal know-how tailored just for you

Recipe Creation Exercise

Ingredients

Choose 2–3 herbs based on your health needs and preferences. Examples are chamomile for relaxation, peppermint for digestion, and lemon balm for mood support.

Form

Decide on the form of your potion: tea, tincture, or infused oil.

Preparation Steps

Tea:

1. Measure 1–2 teaspoons of each selected herb and place them in a teapot or infuser.

2. Boil water and pour it over the herbs.

3. Let the herbs steep for 5–10 minutes, depending on the desired strength.

4. Strain the tea and enjoy it warm or chilled.

Tincture:

1. Fill a glass jar halfway with your chosen herbs.

2. Cover the herbs with alcohol (such as vodka or brandy) until fully submerged.

3. Seal the jar tightly and store it in a cool, dark place for 4–6 weeks, shaking it occasionally.

4. After the steeping period, strain the liquid through a fine mesh strainer or cheesecloth.

5. Pour the tincture into a dark glass bottle and label it with the herb's name and date.

Infused Oil:

1. Fill a glass jar halfway with your selected herbs.

2. Cover the herbs with a carrier oil such as olive or almond oil, ensuring they are fully submerged.

3. Seal the jar tightly and place it on a sunny windowsill for 2–4 weeks, gently shaking it daily.

4. After the infusion period, strain the oil through a fine mesh strainer or cheesecloth.

5. Transfer the infused oil into a dark glass bottle and label it with the herb's name and date.

You're an Alchemist

Get ready to unleash your inner alchemist! You've just unlocked the secrets of turning ordinary herbs into superpowered remedies. Now, let's sprinkle some herbal magic into your daily routine!

Consider how these potions can zap away those pesky health issues as we continue. In the next chapter, we'll whip up some easy-peasy remedies for everyday problems using the magic of herbs. So stick around, keep reading, and let's brew up some wellness together! It's like cooking but with a sprinkle of herbal goodness!

Chapter 7

GENERAL WELLNESS

Have you ever considered using natural remedies to ease your everyday health problems? Well, wonder no more because the answers are right here. Daily everyday struggles can be soothed with the powerful potential of simple herbs. These everyday herbs can become your best allies. This chapter is your guide to a world of natural solutions, showing you how to use herbal remedies for healing. As you explore, you'll learn which herbs work best for specific conditions and be inspired by success stories rooted in the ancient wisdom of herbal wellness.

Unlock the Herbal Arsenal: A Simple Guide to Natural Remedies for Everyday Health Issues

Nature's got many goodies to help with all sorts of health issues. Here's a list of common ailments and herbs that can help you feel better. Whether they're the well-known heroes or the underdogs, these herbal buddies are here to save the day.

Ailments and Their Herbal Sidekicks

Respiratory

- Lagundi (Chinese chaste tree) helps relieve coughs and colds.

- Yerba buena and echinacea boost the immune system and fight infections.

- Elderberries reduce the severity and duration of colds and flu.

- Ginger soothes sore throats and relieves congestion.

- Eucalyptus and peppermint are excellent for treating sinusitis.

Circulatory

- Garlic helps with high blood pressure. (Your breath might scare people, but your heart will thank you!)

- Hawthorn berry and ginkgo improve poor circulation.

Digestive

- Ngai camphor helps relieve diarrhea and abdominal pain.

- Guava leaves are effective in treating diarrhea and stomach issues.

- Peppermint soothes digestion.

- Ginger relieves nausea and promotes digestion.

- Chamomile calms the stomach and reduces bloating.

Hepatobiliary

- Milk thistle and dandelion root detoxify the liver. (Your liver will be as good as new!)

Urinary

- Cranberry and uva ursi help with UTI.
- Chanca piedra helps treat and prevent kidney stones. (Get ready to break those stones like a champ!)

Immune or Lymphatic

- Astragalus and reishi mushrooms boost immunity.

Nervous

- Valerian root and passionflower help with stress and anxiety.
- Feverfew reduces and eases muscle pain.
- Butterbur helps reduce inflammation and lessens the frequency and severity of migraines.
- Lagundi helps reduce inflammation and relieve pain, effectively treating migraines and respiratory issues.
- Yerba buena helps ease toothache and alleviate headaches.
- Lavender calms tension headaches.
- Peppermint relaxes muscles and eases pain.
- Ginger helps with nausea.

Endocrine

- Bitter melon helps lower blood sugar levels (nature's blood sugar buddy).
- Ashwagandha and bladderwrack support thyroid health by balancing thyroid hormone levels.

Musculoskeletal

- Turmeric and boswellia help with arthritis.

- Valerian root and magnesium help with muscle spasms.

- Lagundi is good for sprains and contusions.

Integumentary (Skin)

- Tea tree oil helps with bacterial infections and acne.

- Aloe vera soothes burns and skin irritations.

- Oregon grape helps with psoriasis.

- Calendula heals wounds and reduces inflammation.

- Lagundi is good for dermatitis, scabies, ulcers, and eczema.

- Emperor's candlestick is antifungal against tinea, ringworm, athlete's foot, and scabies.

- Rangoon creeper (Burma creeper) is an anthelminthic (kills parasites such as worms).

- Lagundi and yerba buena help with insect bites.

- Guava leaves cleanse wounds.

Joint Pain and Inflammation

- Turmeric has anti-inflammatory effects.

- Boswellia relieves arthritis symptoms.

- Devil's claw has pain-relieving properties.

Reproductive

- Ginger, chamomile, and yerba buena help with menstrual cramps

- Black cohosh and dong quai reduce menopausal symptoms.

Metabolic

- Green tea and garcinia cambogia help with weight management.

Additional Common Ailments and Remedies

Insomnia

- Valerian root Improves sleep quality.
- Chamomile promotes relaxation and better sleep.
- Lavender reduces anxiety and aids in falling asleep.

Stress and Anxiety

- Ashwagandha reduces stress and anxiety levels.
- Lemon balm calms the nervous system.
- Passionflower reduces anxiety and improves sleep.

Sore Throat

- Licorice root soothes and reduces inflammation.
- Slippery elm provides relief from irritation.
- Marshmallow root eases throat pain.

High Blood Pressure

- Hibiscus lowers blood pressure.
- Garlic improves cardiovascular health.
- Olive leaf supports heart health.

Allergies

- Butterbur reduces hay fever symptoms.
- Stinging nettle is a natural antihistamine.
- Quercetin reduces allergic reactions.

Memory and Concentration

- Ginkgo enhances cognitive function.
- Rosemary boosts memory and concentration.
- Gotu kola improves mental clarity.

Herbal Heroes: How Nature's Remedies Changed My Life

Earlier in this book, I mentioned how herbs have dramatically transformed my health. Now, it's time to dive deeper into my journey and share how these simple, natural remedies have become my everyday heroes.

Living with multiple sclerosis, an incurable chronic disease, has its fair share of challenges. The fatigue, the muscle spasms, and the constant balancing act of not only walking but also managing symptoms—all of it can feel overwhelming. However, discovering the power of herbs has given me a new lease on life, helping me cope with daily struggles and become a lot healthier without relying solely on traditional pharmaceutical drugs.

My Herbal Allies

Energy Boosters

Fatigue is a constant companion with multiple sclerosis, but a particular herb has helped me reclaim some of my energy.

- Ashwagandha every other day helps me fight fatigue.

Muscle Spasms and Pain Relief

Muscle spasms and pain were once my daily tormentors, but these herbs have offered significant relief:

- Cayenne pepper works wonders for calming muscle spasms when used in a salve. It's like a gentle, natural muscle relaxant, especially when overexerting myself.

- Turmeric has anti-inflammatory properties that have been essential in reducing pain and inflammation in my joints and muscles.

Immune Support

With multiple sclerosis, keeping my immune system in check is crucial. I sue these herbs to help support a balanced immune response:

- Echinacea boosts my immune system and helps ward off infections. I do not take this regularly since I don't want my immune system to kick into overload due to my illness.
- Reishi mushroom strengthens my immune defenses, making me more resilient against illnesses.

Stress and Anxiety

Living with a chronic condition can be mentally taxing. These herbs help keep me calm and centered:

- Chamomile reduces my stress and anxiety levels, helping me stay calm even on challenging days.
- Lemon balm, which I usually have as a tea, calms my nervous system and promotes peace, making my days more manageable.

Cognitive Clarity

Brain fog can be a real struggle, but these herbs have sharpened my mental focus:

- Lion's mane mushroom keeps my brain healthy, which I take daily.
- Rosemary boosts my concentration and mental clarity, making everyday tasks less daunting.

Digestive Health

Digestive issues often accompany chronic illness, but this herb keeps my gut happy:

- Ginger relieves nausea and promotes healthy digestion, making me feel more comfortable. I will sometimes substitute peppermint for an upset stomach in place of ginger.

Sleep and Relaxation

Quality sleep is essential for healing, and these herbs have helped improve my sleep:

- Valerian promotes relaxation and better sleep which helps me wake up refreshed.

- Lavender reduces anxiety and aids in falling asleep, ensuring I get the rest I need. Sprayed on my pillow and sheets or in a sachet under my pillow usually works for me.

Coping With Other Daily Ailments

Daily life dealing with health woes means managing a variety of symptoms, and herbs have been invaluable in this process:

- Colds and flu: Whenever I'm catching a cold, I increase my garlic intake by cooking with it and taking a spoonful of honey-infused garlic or adding a spoonful of lemon ginger-infused honey to an elderberry tea.

- Coughs and sinuses: I usually take a few drops of a mullein tincture in my water.

- Sore throat: Marshmallow root tincture gets added to the drops of mullein tincture mix, as my sore throat and sinus issues seem to go hand in hand.

Herbs have become my everyday allies, helping me manage my chronic disease and improve my overall well-being. They've offered a natural, gentle way to cope with symptoms, boosting my energy, reducing pain, supporting my immune system, and enhancing my mental clarity. I've found a balance that allows me to rely less on traditional pharmaceutical drugs and embrace the healing power of nature. They've improved my life, and I hope they can do the same for you. Whether you're dealing with a chronic condition like mine or just looking for natural ways to boost your health, these herbal heroes are here to help you every step of the way.

Herbal Traditions: A Story of Health and Heritage

Our journey together explored how herbs transformed my life, providing relief and wellness where conventional medicine fell short. Let's now turn to the broader narrative of herb use in communities where traditions and modernity intertwine.

Shared Wisdom and Community Knowledge

Both African Americans and Caucasians use traditional and store-bought herbs equally, but it's usually the women who turn to these natural remedies more often. This herbal knowledge is passed down through generations, like family secrets. Imagine an elderly African American man saying, "We learn from our heritage, from generation to generation" (Altizer et al., 2011).

Take this story: An older woman heard her niece complaining about hot flashes. She told her, "Get some sage and sugar, put it in a bag, and tuck it under your tongue until it dissolves." Simple, old-school advice like this is pure gold in these communities.

Mixing the Old With the New

Older adults mix traditional wisdom with new information from books, magazines, the internet, and YouTube videos like *Eye on Health*. One woman said, "You just have to read. The media is a big source." However, they're careful about what they believe. Some users of herbs have warned, "Some herbs are just artificial. You never know if it's right or wrong. You just take a chance" (Altizer et al., 2011).

Using herbs is all about mixing traditional wisdom with new knowledge. It's not about ditching modern medicine but complementing it. This approach highlights the importance of understanding each person's unique health practices and cultural background.

How Herbs Help

Herbs have different roles in managing health. Traditional herbs like yellowroot, aloe vera, and chamomile are great for quick fixes like upset stomachs or trouble sleeping. Just picture a woman sipping chamomile tea to drift off to sleep like her grandma did before her.

On the other hand, commercial herbs like goldenseal and Echinacea are used for long-term health and boosting the immune system. In a study on herb use in multiethnic adults, one African American woman mentioned using Echinacea drops with goldenseal to stay healthy (Arcury et al., 2007).

Practical and Personal Reasons

Choosing herbs is often about saving money and avoiding the hassle of doctor visits. There are many remedies people used to do in the past that we can still use today. Herbs are often the go-to when regular medicine doesn't work. One participant said, "I take what I think is good for me. When I get sick, the first thing I think of is finding an herb" (Altizer et al., 2011).

As we wrap up, remember that herbs are powerful for their healing properties and the stories and traditions they carry. These herbal heroes continue to support and heal, weaving a tale of resilience, knowledge, and community across generations.

Unleashing the Secret Powers of Everyday Herbs

We've all heard of lemon balm, echinacea, and St. John's wort. They're like the superheroes of the herb world, right? But these herbal Avengers have secret identities with powers you might not know about. Let's dive into their lesser-known talents and discover fun, new ways to use them.

Lemon Balm: More Than a Sleepy-Time Hero

Lemon balm is famous for helping us relax and ease stress, but it has a few other tricks up its leafy sleeves:

- Cold sore zapper: Got a cold sore? Lemon balm can help kick it to the curb. Just dab a bit of lemon balm extract on the sore a few times daily. Boom! Cold sore, be gone.

- Brain booster: Need a mental pick-me-up? Lemon balm can help with that, too. Add fresh leaves to your tea or salad, and watch your focus and memory get sharper.

- Digestive dynamo: Feeling bloated? Lemon balm can soothe your tummy troubles. Brew a simple tea by steeping the leaves in hot water for 10 minutes and sip before meals.

Echinacea: Not Just for Fighting Colds

Echinacea is the go-to herb for boosting your immune system, but did you know it can do more?

- Skin savior: Echinacea can treat eczema, psoriasis, and minor wounds. Mix it with coconut oil and apply it to trouble spots to make a home-made salve.

- Inflammation fighter: Echinacea can reduce inflammation throughout your body. Sprinkle the dried herb into your soups and stews, or take it as a tincture to avoid inflammation.

- Oral health helper: Echinacea keeps your gums and teeth happy. Mix a few drops of echinacea tincture in water to make a mouthwash. Rinse twice a day for a healthier smile.

St. John's Wort: More Than a Mood Lifter

St. John's wort is well-known for helping with depression and anxiety, but it has a few more tricks:

- Menstrual marvel: Are you struggling with cramps? St. John's wort tea can help ease the pain. Drink a cup during your period for some sweet relief.

- Wound warrior: This herb can speed up the healing of cuts, scrapes, and burns. Apply St. John's wort oil to your wounds and watch them heal faster.

- Sun shield: Believe it or not, St. John's wort can help protect your skin from sun damage. Make a St. John's wort-infused oil and apply it before you head out into the sun.

Fun and Creative Ways to Use Herbs

- Herbal ice cubes: Freeze lemon balm, echinacea, or St. John's wort in ice cube trays. Pop these herbal ice cubes into your drinks for a refreshing twist.

- Herbal steams: Open up your pores and rejuvenate your skin with an herbal steam. Boil water, add a handful of herbs, and lean over the steam with a towel over your head. Spa day at home, anyone?

- Herbal oils: Infuse oils with these herbs for a multipurpose solution. Use the oils for cooking, skincare, or as a base for homemade salves and lotions.

The Magic of Versatility

The real magic of these herbs is their ability to do so much more than we give them credit for. By exploring these lesser-known uses, you can get the most out of lemon balm, echinacea, St. John's wort, and other herbs in your everyday life. These herbs are like Swiss Army knives for your health.

So, don't be afraid to experiment with these new uses. You'll boost your herbal knowledge and find personalized ways to stay healthy naturally. Let these herbal remedies bring new vitality and wellness into your life, one leaf at a time.

Ailment–Herb: Interactive Element

We have learned about herbs that can help with common illnesses. Are you ready to test your knowledge? If so, take a look at the table below and match the herbs with the illnesses they treat.

Herbs	Remedies
Turmeric	Helps relieve coughs and colds
Peppermint	Lowers blood pressure
Lagundi	Has anti-inflammatory effects
Aloe vera	Enhances cognitive function
Reishi mushroom	Improves sleep quality
Ashwagandha	Relaxes muscles and eases pain
Hibiscus	Soothes burns and skin irritation
Ginkgo	Boosts immunity

Wrapping Up

This chapter taught us about using basic herbs to treat common ailments. We also discussed the extra advantages of herbs like lemon balm and how they've helped many people, including myself. Now, as we finish discussing using herbs for healing, let's look ahead to see how we can easily include these remedies in our daily routines. In the next chapter, we'll see how to integrate herbal treatments into your daily life smoothly.

Chapter 8

UTILIZING HERBALISM

Imagine starting your day with nature's touch, where herbs heal and enhance your day. From the interesting discussions we've had, it's evident that herbs can seamlessly be incorporated into our daily lives. So, not only can we imagine it, but we can easily turn interacting with nature into a reality. This chapter is your guide to making herbal remedies a joyful and rejuvenating part of your everyday routine.

Practical Tips for Incorporating Herbal Remedies into Your Daily Wellness Routine

The world of herbs is filled with various herbal remedies that can become an invaluable addition to your everyday routine. Here are some easy and practical ways to include them in your morning or bedtime routines:

Morning Routine

Start Your Day with Herbal Teas

- Lemon balm tea for calmness

Begin your morning with a soothing cup of lemon balm tea. Known for its calming properties, lemon balm helps reduce morning anxiety and sets a serene tone for the day. It has been used to reduce stress and anxiety since the Middle Ages.

- Peppermint tea for energy

If you're looking for a refreshing start, try peppermint tea. It wakes you up and invigorates your senses without the need for caffeine. Ancient Egyptians and Greeks valued peppermint for its ability to boost energy and alleviate digestive issues.

Add Herbs to Your Breakfast

- Turmeric smoothie

A turmeric smoothie is another terrific way to kick-start your day. Adding a teaspoon of this golden spice to your blend of fruits, yogurt, and honey can provide anti-inflammatory benefits and a unique flavor. Turmeric has been used in Ayurvedic medicine for thousands of years for its healing properties.

- Herb-infused oatmeal

If you enjoy oatmeal, enhance it with a sprinkle of cinnamon or ginger. These spices aid digestion and add a delightful, warming taste.

Using Herbs in Cooking

- Rosemary, thyme, and basil

Incorporate herbs like rosemary, thyme, basil, and parsley into your meals besides breakfast. They not only enhance the flavor but also offer numerous health benefits. Herbs have been essential in culinary traditions worldwide, dating back to ancient civilizations, for their flavor and medicinal uses.

Herbal Essential Oils for Focus

As you gear up for a productive day, consider using essential oils to boost your concentration.

- Peppermint oil for concentration

Keep a small bottle of peppermint essential oil at your desk. A quick sniff or a dab on your temples can sharpen your focus and enhance your concentration.

Bedtime Routine

Herbal Teas for Relaxation

- Chamomile tea for sleep

Unwind with a cup of chamomile tea about an hour before bed. This herb helps relax your mind and prepares your body for a good night's sleep. Chamomile has been a popular remedy since ancient Egypt, where it was used for its calming effects.

- Lavender tea for stress relief

Brew a cup of lavender tea to melt away stress and tension, making it easier to drift into a peaceful slumber. Lavender has been used since Roman times for its soothing scent and ability to reduce stress.

Herbal Bath Soaks

Imagine ending your day with a luxurious soak in an herbal bath. Being highly absorbent, your skin takes in the medicinal benefits of the herbs while you relax. Let the calming aroma and soothing properties of the herbs wash over you. It's like having a spa right in your home!

- Lavender bath

Enhance your bath with a few drops of essential oil or a handful of dried lavender flowers. It's a fantastic way to relax your muscles and mind before bedtime. Romans were known to add lavender to their baths to benefit from its calming properties.

- Epsom salt with herbs

Epsom salts, named after a saline spring in Epsom, England, have been used for centuries for their therapeutic benefits. Mixing Epsom salts with dried herbs like chamomile or rosemary may offer a soothing and detoxifying bath experience.

Ways to Incorporate Medicinal Herbs Into Your Daily Routine

Evening Tea Ritual

As the day winds down, there's nothing like a warm cup of tea to help you relax. Picture this: You sit down, take a deep breath, and enjoy 15 minutes of pure calm as you sip a soothing herbal tea. This evening ritual helps your body physically unwind and tells your brain it's time to relax and get ready for sleep. Herbs like peppermint, lemon balm, passionflower, and milky oat tops are perfect for this nighttime routine.

Aromatherapy

A simple sniff can genuinely transform your day. Bring a small bottle of essential oils like peppermint, citrus, or rosemary. Whenever you feel stressed or need a mental boost, take a whiff. These aromatic herbs can quickly clear your head, helping you stay relaxed yet focused.

Simple Salves

Salves are your portable herbal remedy. Made from herbal oil infusions, they're great for healing and moisturizing skin. Use them for irritated skin, lip balms, or first aid. Keep a small tin in your bag for quick relief wherever you are.

Herbal Bitters

If your digestion needs a little help, herbal bitters are your friend. A quick spritz on your tongue before a meal can stimulate digestive enzymes and prepare your stomach for optimal digestion. They're easy to use—just a few drops or a spray about 10 minutes before eating can make an enormous difference. Urban Moonshine offers some great options to try. Eating a salad before the meal can also do the trick, as most salad greens fall into the bitter category. Have you ever noticed that restaurants usually offer a salad before the meal? I like to think that this is why. Also, that piece of parsley that sits there on the plate and is hardly ever eaten? It's for digestion also.

By weaving these simple herbal practices into your daily routine, you'll discover medicinal herbs' gentle yet powerful benefits. From calming your mind in the evening to boosting your digestion, these natural remedies enhance your daily well-being.

Personalized Herbal Regimen

Consult a professional: Speak with a healthcare provider or herbalist to determine which herbs may benefit your health needs. They can help you create a personalized herbal regimen.

By incorporating these simple tips into your daily routines, you can harness the power of herbs to support your overall health and well-being naturally. Enjoy the journey to a more balanced and healthier you!

Herbs for Skin Care, Hair Care, and Beauty: The Beauty Enthusiasts' Complete Guide

Let's dive into the world of natural, gentle beauty treatments that have been cherished for centuries and can elevate your skin and hair routine.

Yellow Sweet Clover: The King's Clover

Did you know that Henry VIII loved yellow sweet clover? Yep, it was even called King's Clover! This herb works wonders for red, dry skin, leaving your face radiant, youthful, and with a nice, even tone.

Lavender: The Relaxing Healer

Lavender isn't just for making your room smell nice or helping you sleep better. This herb has natural antiseptic properties and helps boost circulation, supporting your skin's natural healing process. Plus, it's super relaxing—just what you need after a long day.

Chamomile: The Calm and Soothing Daisy

Chamomile is another herb that helps you relax, just like lavender. Yet, did you know it also has regenerative and soothing properties? It's great for repairing your skin, making it look and feel fantastic.

Echinacea: The Immune Booster

You might know echinacea as a cold and flu fighter, but it does so much more! This herb enhances your skin's natural immunity and protects against environmental stressors. It's like a little shield for your face.

Comfrey: The Ancient Healer

Comfrey has been used for over 2,000 years in traditional medicine, especially in Japan. Its roots and leaves are packed with goodness that's great for your skin.

Thyme: The Anti-Acne Warrior

Thyme isn't just for cooking; it has antifungal, anti-inflammatory, and antibacterial properties. An article in Healthcare Business Today (2021) states that a study conducted in the UK even suggests it fights pimples better than popular anti-acne products. Say goodbye to breakouts with this powerful herb!

Peppermint: The Cool Refresher

Peppermint is more than a fresh scent. It's an antioxidant that relaxes your mind, body, and skin. This ancient herb is excellent for cooling and refreshing your skin, leaving you feeling rejuvenated.

Rosemary: The Ageless Wonder

Rosemary is a must-have for your beauty routine. It helps with everything from digestion to lowering blood pressure. Its anti-inflammatory and astringent properties for your skin slow aging and eliminate free radical damage. Talk about a multitasker!

Aloe Vera: The Hydration Ally

Apply aloe vera gel to your face before bed. It's fabulous for soothing and hydrating your skin overnight.

Calendula Cream: The Healer

If you have dry or irritated skin, moisturize and heal it with a calendula-infused cream before you sleep. Calendula is a powerhouse for skin issues.

Easy DIY Herbal Beauty Treatments

Ready to try these herbs at home? Here are some simple recipes:

Lavender–Chamomile Relaxing Face Mask

Ingredients:

- 1 tablespoon dried lavender
- 1 tablespoon dried chamomile
- 2 tablespoons honey

1 tablespoon yogurt

Instructions:

1. Grind the lavender and chamomile into a fine powder.
2. Mix with honey and yogurt.
3. Apply to your face and leave for 15 minutes.
4. Rinse with warm water for smooth, calm skin.

Peppermint–Rosemary Hair Rinse

Ingredients:

1 tablespoon dried peppermint

1 tablespoon dried rosemary

2 cups boiling water

Instructions:

1. Steep the herbs in boiling water for 20 minutes.
2. Strain and let cool.
3. After shampooing, pour the rinse over your hair and leave it in for soft, silky hair.

Yellow Sweet Clover Soothing Bath Soak

Ingredients:

1 cup dried yellow sweet clover

1 cup Epsom salt

a muslin bag or old pantyhose

Instructions:

1. Place the sweet clover and Epsom salt in the muslin bag.
2. Hang the bag under the faucet as you fill your tub.

3. Soak in the warm bath for 20 minutes.

4. Relax and let your skin soak up the goodness!

Why These Treatments Work

These herbal beauty treatments are gentle and natural, perfect for all skin types, especially for seniors. They're packed with healing properties without the harsh chemicals found in many commercial products. Try them and let nature's beauty secrets transform your skin and hair.

Now, go ahead and embrace the power of herbs in your beauty routine. Your skin and hair will be thankful!

Nature's Remedies: Herbs for Mental Health and Stress Relief

Let's discuss how some marvelous herbs can help you relax, unwind, and tackle stress like a pro. Grab a comfy seat, and let's dive into the world of herbal magic for mental health and stress relief.

Lavender: The Relaxation Champion

Lavender is like a warm hug in a plant. Traditionally, it's been used to help you relax and calm down, making it great for easing anxiety and even PTSD. Picture this: After a long day, you light a lavender-scented candle, breathe in the soothing aroma, and feel your stress melt away; the perfect way to end the day.

Ashwagandha: The Stress Buster

Ashwagandha, also known as *Withania somnifera*, is a superstar in the herb world. This powerful plant can help reduce anxiety and depression. It's packed with goodies that beat stress, fight fatigue, and have anti-inflammatory benefits. Imagine taking a daily ashwagandha supplement and feeling more balanced and calmer as the days pass.

Passionflower: The Relaxation Expert

Passionflower, or *Passiflora incarnata*, is your go-to herb for fighting anxiety and promoting relaxation. It's also helpful for those annoying menopausal symptoms like hot flashes. Think about sipping on a warm cup of passionflower tea in the evening and feeling the day's worries drift away.

Holy Basil (Tulsi): The Stress Warrior

Holy basil, also known as tulsi, is rich in antioxidants, making it perfect for tackling stress, anxiety, and depression. Visualize adding a few tulsi leaves to your tea and feel a wave of calmness wash over you with each sip. In India, tulsi is considered a sacred plant often grown in homes for its spiritual benefits.

Chamomile: The Gentle Soother

Chamomile is like nature's little tranquilizer. It's loaded with phenolics like flavonoids and antioxidants that help reduce stress and ease you into a peaceful night's sleep without a care in the world.

Valerian Root: The Sleep Saver

Valerian root is a classic for dealing with insomnia and anxiety. Be careful, though—it can sometimes cause headaches or dizziness, so moderation is key.

Brahmi: The Memory Booster

Brahmi is fantastic for relieving stress and anxiety and is also known for boosting memory. Consider incorporating Brahmi into your daily routine; you may notice your stress levels drop while your focus sharpens.

Bonus Herbs for Mental Health

- Lemon balm: This herb reduces anxiety and promotes calmness. Adding fresh lemon balm leaves to your water or tea will make you feel more re-laxed.

- St. John's wort: Known for its antidepressant qualities, this herb can help lift your spirits. Imagine taking St. John's wort supplements and feeling a subtle boost in your mood over time.

How to Use These Herbs

- Teas: Steep your favorite herbs in hot water for a soothing drink. For example, make a calming blend with lavender, chamomile, and passion-flower.

- Baths: Add a handful of dried herbs, such as lavender or chamomile, to your bath for a relaxing soak. To avoid a mess, you can also use a muslin bag.

- Aromatherapy: Use essential oils from these herbs in a diffuser to fill your space with calming scents. Lavender and peppermint are excellent choices for this.

Earlier in the book, I alluded to the stress and herbs I took to combat it. In time, I grew to understand the importance of physical and mental health. I noticed a drastic change once I became serious about my herbal journey. My anxiety and stress lessened, and I became more relaxed.

Oftentimes, just the simple act of brewing teas may be enough to provide a moment of peace. By incorporating these wonderful herbs into your daily routine, you can enjoy their calming and stress-relieving properties and improve your overall mental well-being. So go ahead and explore these herbal remedies and find the perfect blend that works for you.

Herbal Wellness Journaling

Journaling has often become a fantastic outlet for expressing one's thoughts and feelings on paper. It can also be a wonderful way to keep track of one's herbal journey experience.

Different Ways to Journal

According to an article done by Gaia Herbs, there are several ways to journal, for instance:

- **Bullet journaling:** Create a to-do list to organize tasks you want to do regarding your herbal journey and clear your mind. This is especially helpful at night to manage thoughts that keep you awake.

- **Collage journaling:** Combine photos of herbs you see, observations you've made, and your writings or drawings. It's like scrapbooking and allows you to express yourself creatively.

- **Life events or seasons journaling:** Write about whether you're entering a season of trying new herbal remedies and your experiences.

Journaling is quite beneficial in helping you keep track of any changes in your mood. According to Gaia Herbs, it can also reduce blood pressure and improve mindfulness and other aspects of mental health (Boye, 2023).

Winding Down

Together, we've explored ways to incorporate herbs into our lives. From morning routines filled with herbal teas and more nutritional meals to skin care—herbs can do it all. They offer not only physical enhancements but cater to our mental health as well. As you begin exploring natural remedies, journaling is one of the best hobbies to pick up to ensure you never miss a thing on this fascinating journey in a world where nature is just an arm's reach away.

In the next chapter, we'll delve deeper into the specialized applications of these natural wonders. We'll uncover the specific uses of herbs in treating targeted health concerns, further expanding our herbal horizons.

Chapter 9

INDIVIDUALIZED HERBAL CARE

In life, we each have unique needs that deserve attention. Finding tailored solutions that truly cater to your requirements can be challenging. Still, have you considered the remarkable ability of herbs to address specific health concerns, such as hormone balance and immunity boosting? This chapter delves into the fascinating realm of herbal remedies, illustrating how the gifts of nature can be customized to suit your health requirements.

Nature's Secrets: Herbal Remedies for Women's Health and Hormonal Harmony

Imagine a garden of healing just waiting to be discovered that contains remedies for women's health and hormonal balance. Let's stroll through this garden and engage with the familiar herbs that can help you feel your best.

Ashwagandha Tea

Ashwagandha is like the Zen master of herbs. It helps reduce stress and balance your hormones. Imagine having a little yoga instructor in a cup! To take ashwagandha, you can make a calming tea.

Ingredients:

1 teaspoon ashwagandha powder

1 cup hot water

Instruction:

Steep the powder in hot water for 10 minutes, strain, and sip your way to serenity.

Black Cohosh Tincture

Black cohosh is the wise grandmother of herbs. She's been soothing menopausal symptoms like hot flashes and mood swings for centuries. It's like chatting with a wise elder; typically, you take it as a tincture.

Ingredient:

30 drops of the tincture

Instruction:

Pour the tincture into a glass of water. Drink up and feel those hot flashes cool down.

Chasteberry Tea

Chasteberry is the dependable best friend you need during PMS. It helps balance your menstrual cycle and ease PMS symptoms. Enjoy this as a comforting tea.

Ingredients:

1 teaspoon dried chasteberry

1 cup boiling water

Instruction:

Steep the berries for 10 minutes and enjoy a soothing cup of relief.

Dandelion Root Tea

Dandelion Root is like the detox specialist of the herb world. It supports liver health, which is crucial for hormonal balance. Think of it as giving your liver a refreshing spa day, so make a detoxifying tea.

Ingredients:

>   1 tablespoon dried dandelion root
>
>   1 cup water

Instruction:

>   Simmer the root in water for 10 minutes, strain, and drink to give your liver some love.

Maca Smoothie

Maca is the energizer bunny of herbs. It boosts energy and libido and balances hormones. Add a teaspoon of maca powder to your smoothies, oatmeal, or coffee.

Ingredients:

>   1 teaspoon maca powder
>
>   1 banana
>
>   1 cup milk (any kind)
>
>   a handful of spinach

Instruction:

>   Blend and feel that extra pep in your step!

Milk Thistle Tea

Milk thistle is the liver's loyal bodyguard. It detoxifies and protects, ensuring your liver can help keep hormones in check. Brew a protective tea.

Ingredients:

>   1 teaspoon crushed milk thistle seeds
>
>   1 cup boiling water

Instruction:

Steep for 20 minutes and drink to shield your liver.

Motherwort Tincture

Motherwort is like a warm hug from Mom. It calms anxiety and soothes menstrual cramps. Please take it as a tincture.

Ingredient:

30 drops of the tincture

Instruction:

Pour the tincture into a glass of water, and drink whenever you need a comforting hug.

Red Raspberry Leaf Tea

Red raspberry leaf is the ultimate helper for reproductive health. It tones the uterus and eases menstrual discomfort. It also makes a lovely tea.

Ingredients:

1 tablespoon dried red raspberry leaves

1 cup hot water

Instruction:

Steep for 10 minutes and enjoy it like a cozy chat with your best friend.

Evening Primrose Oil

Evening primrose oil is excellent for skin health and easing PMS. Take it in capsule form for a skin glow-up.

Fenugreek Tea

Fenugreek helps boost milk production for breastfeeding moms. Make a nourishing tea.

Ingredients:

1 teaspoon fenugreek seeds

1 cup boiling water

Instruction:

Steep 10 minutes, strain, and drink to support milk flow.

St. John's Wort Tea

St. John's wort lifts spirits and eases mild depression. It's like bottled sunshine. Please take it as tea or tincture.

Ingredients:

1 teaspoon dried St. John's wort

1 cup hot water

Instruction:

Steep for 10 minutes and let the sunshine in.

Remember, always talk to a healthcare provider before starting any new herbal routine, especially if you have underlying health conditions or are on medication. Here's to happy, healthy herbal healing!

Guarding the Golden Years: Boosting Your Immune System

Getting older comes with its own set of challenges, especially when it comes to our immune system. Our body's natural defense against illnesses doesn't work as well as it used to, making us more likely to catch things like colds and flu.

Nature's Medicine Cabinet: The Power of Herbs

Don't worry—nature has some tricks up its sleeve! Herbs have been boosting health for centuries and can help seniors keep their immune systems strong in various ways.

Cooking With Herbs

Your kitchen is one of the best places to prepare different ways to consume herbal remedies. Herbs like turmeric, ginger, cinnamon, and garlic are perfect additions to your meals, adding flavor and saving the day.

Use these herbs in soups, stews, curries, or stir-fries. They will not only add unique flavor but also boost your immune system.

Herbal Teas

Picture yourself with a cozy cup of tea, feeling the warm touch of good health. Try teas made from echinacea, peppermint, or elderberry. It's a relaxing way to support your immune system and stay hydrated.

Smoothies

Think of smoothies as your secret weapon. You can sneak all kinds of good stuff in there! Add herbs like ginger, turmeric, or ashwagandha to your smoothies. They'll give you an extra health kick without you even noticing.

Supplements

If you're always on the go, herbal supplements might be your best sidekick. Take herbal supplements in the form of capsules, tablets, or tinctures. Just be sure to check with a healthcare professional first.

Topical Applications

Some herbs can work wonders on your skin and through the air. Use essential oils like oregano and holy basil. Dilute them with a carrier oil and apply them to your skin, or pop them in a diffuser and unlock instant relaxation.

Herbal Baths

Add herbs like lavender, chamomile, or rosemary to your bathwater to turn bath time into a wellness retreat. It's like a relaxing and immune-boosting soak all in one.

Gardening

Why not grow your herbal heroes? Plant herbs in a garden or pots on your windowsill. You'll have a fresh supply right at your fingertips, plus the joy of gardening.

Aromatherapy

Let's not forget the power of scent. Use essential oils from herbs like lavender, peppermint, or eucalyptus in a diffuser or as a room spray. Create a calming, health-promoting environment and sniff your way into good health.

Additional Herbs to Boost Your Immune System

- Turmeric is like a shining knight in golden armor, ready to fight off inflammation. Add it to soups, stews, or smoothies, and let its superpower, curcumin, keep you feeling spry.

- Echinacea is your trusty shield against colds and flu, like a bodyguard keeping the germs at bay. Sip on echinacea tea to stay protected.

- Ginger is the spicy, zingy hero that boosts digestion and immunity. It's like the spicy best friend who always knows how to help. Use it in teas or add it to your meals for a health boost.

- Cinnamon is not just a sweet spice; it's a protector that balances blood sugar and fights off bacteria. Sprinkle it on your oatmeal or in your coffee for a tasty shield.

- Peppermint is a refreshing herb that clears up congestion faster than you can say "ahhh." Its

menthol makes breathing easier, so drink peppermint tea when stuffed up.

- Astragalus has been used for centuries as a long-
term immune booster, like an ancient shield. Add
astragalus root to soups, or take it as a supplement.

- Paprika is a colorful spice packed with vitamins,
especially vitamin C. It gives your immune system a bright, spicy boost. Sprinkle it on eggs,
veggies, or meats, and enjoy the extra flavor and
health benefits.

Keeping your immune system strong in your senior years
means looking at the whole picture: eating right, staying
active, getting enough sleep, and managing stress. Herbs
are a natural, effective way to give your immune system a
little extra help. By making these powerful plants part of
your daily routine, you can stay healthy and enjoy your
golden years with energy and vitality. So let these herbs
work their magic, and enjoy the benefits of a boosted
immune system.

Herbal Harmony: Natural Solutions for Digestive Health and Pain Relief

Maintaining digestive health can become more challenging as we age. Seniors often experience issues such as
slower digestion, constipation, and bloating. These problems can arise due to decreased stomach acid production,
less physical activity, and changes in diet. Additionally,
many older adults take medications that can affect their
digestive system, leading to discomfort and irregular
bowel movements.

Pain, whether from arthritis, muscle strain, or other
conditions, can also become more common. These challenges can make everyday life more difficult, but natural

remedies, like certain herbs, can help improve digestive health and relieve pain.

Ginger: The Spicy Champion

Ginger is one of the spicy herbs in the herbal world. It is known far and wide for calming upset stomachs and easing nausea. It is like the friendly neighbor who always has a remedy for everything. Ginger's anti-inflammatory properties can also help with pain.

How to use ginger:

- Ginger tea: Slice a piece of fresh ginger and steep it in hot water for 10 minutes. Add honey and lemon if you like.

- Ginger smoothie: Blend a small piece of fresh ginger into your favorite smoothie for an extra zing and digestive boost.

Peppermint: The Refreshing Soother

Peppermint is a refreshing soother and is perfect for relaxing the digestive system and relieving pain from indigestion or Irritable Bowel Syndrome (IBS).

How to use peppermint:

- Peppermint tea: Steep fresh or dried peppermint leaves in hot water for 5–10 minutes. Sip slowly and feel the relief.

- Peppermint oil: Apply diluted peppermint oil to your temples or abdomen for pain relief.

Fennel: The Gentle Giant

Fennel is known for its ability to ease bloating and gas. It offers the comforting hug you need after a big meal.

How to use fennel:

- Fennel tea: Crush a teaspoon of fennel seeds and steep in hot water for 10 minutes. Strain and enjoy.
- Fennel seeds: Chew on a few fennel seeds after meals to aid digestion.

Turmeric: The Golden Warrior

Then there's turmeric, the golden warrior with a heart of gold. Turmeric's anti-inflammatory powers, as we've come to learn, are legendary, and it helps with digestive discomfort and pain.

How to use turmeric:

- Turmeric milk: Mix a teaspoon of turmeric powder into warm milk. Add a pinch of black pepper and honey for taste.
- Turmeric tea: Boil turmeric root or powder in water for 10 minutes. Strain and drink.

Chamomile: The Gentle Relaxer

Finally, we come to chamomile, the gentle relaxer. Chamomile is perfect for soothing stomach cramps and easing stress-related digestive issues.

How to use chamomile:

- Chamomile tea: Steep chamomile flowers in hot water for 5–10 minutes. Drink before bed for a calming effect.
- Chamomile bath: Add chamomile tea or essential oil to your bathwater for a relaxing soak.

Using Herbal Remedies to Help Manage

Chronic Conditions

Let's discuss how herbs can be helpful buddies in managing chronic conditions. These natural remedies can complement your regular treatments, making it easier to manage long-term health issues.

How Herbs Can Help with Chronic Conditions

They can work alongside your usual medications and treatments to help manage symptoms and improve your overall well-being.

Here's how they can help:

- Reduce inflammation: Herbs like turmeric and ginger have anti-inflammatory properties, which can help reduce pain and swelling in conditions like arthritis.

- Enhance relaxation: Chamomile and lavender can help reduce stress and improve sleep, which is significant for managing chronic conditions.

Some plants can be helpful for chronic conditions because they contain natural compounds that may ease symptoms and improve overall health. These compounds can positively affect the body and help manage long-lasting health issues that will provide the relief you need.

Herbs in Pediatric Care: Nurturing Our

Little Ones Naturally

Many parents prefer natural and gentle remedies for their children's health. Herbs can help with common childhood issues, but using them for kids requires careful thought and following safety guidelines.

Guidelines for Using Herbs Safely in Pediatric Care

Consult a healthcare professional: Always talk to a pediatrician or a qualified herbalist before giving your child any herbal remedies. They can give advice based on your child's specific needs.

Choose child-friendly herbs: Not all herbs are safe for kids. Stick to well-known, gentle herbs that are recognized as safe for children.

Use age-appropriate dosages: Kids aren't just small adults; their bodies handle substances differently. Adjust the dosage according to your child's age and weight.

Avoid certain herbs: Some herbs, like ephedra and goldenseal, and adult essential oils can be too strong or harmful for kids. Always research or get professional advice on which herbs to avoid.

Monitor for allergic reactions: Introduce one herb at a time and watch for signs of an allergic reaction, like rash, itching, or trouble breathing. Stop using the herb immediately if you see any of these signs.

Use proper preparation methods: Herbal teas, alcohol-free tinctures, and syrups are the best ways to give herbs to kids. Capsules and tablets are generally not recommended for younger children.

Educate yourself: Learn about the herbs you plan to use. Reliable resources and professional advice can help you make safe choices.

The Importance of Dosage and Herb Selection for Children

Dosage Matters

The right dosage for kids is essential. One common method is Clark's rule, which adjusts the adult dose based on the child's weight. For example, if the adult dose is 100 milligrams and the child weighs 30 pounds, you divide the child's weight by 150 (the average adult weight in pounds) and then multiply by the adult dose. So $(30 \div 150) \times 100 = 20$. This ensures the dose is safe and effective for a child's smaller body.

Selecting the Right Herbs

- Chamomile tea can help calm a fussy baby or soothe an upset stomach.

- Elderberry syrup boosts the immune system, especially during cold and flu season.

- Ginger can help with nausea and digestive discomfort. Fresh ginger tea with a small amount of honey can be comforting. Do not use honey if the child is under a year old, not even if it is a drop.

- Lavender helps with relaxation and sleep. A few drops of lavender oil in a diffuser can create a calming bedtime environment.

- Echinacea can support the immune system and help fight infections. Use alcohol-free tinctures for kids.

Herbs can be a fantastic, natural way to support your child's health, but safety and proper usage are crucial. Always consult healthcare professionals, use the correct dosages, and choose the best herbs for your child's needs. By following these guidelines, you can safely use the power of herbs to nurture and protect your little ones.

DIY Herbal Remedy Plan

Creating your herbal remedy plan can be a great way to support your health naturally. Here's a simple template to help you get started. This plan includes sections for identifying health goals, selecting appropriate herbs, and planning how to incorporate these herbs into your daily routine.

Step 1: Identify Your Health Goals

Write down your specific health goals. Be as clear and specific as possible. Here are some examples:

- to improve digestion
- to boost the immune system
- to reduce stress and anxiety
- to alleviate joint pain

Step 2: Select Appropriate Herbs

Choose herbs that are known to support your health goals. Research or consult with a healthcare professional to ensure you're selecting the right herbs.

Health goal 1: (e.g., to improve digestion)

- Herb 1: (e.g., ginger)
- Herb 2: (e.g., peppermint)

Health goal 2: (e.g., to boost the immune system)

- Herb 1: (e.g., elderberry)
- Herb 2: (e.g., echinacea)

Health goal 3: (e.g., to reduce stress and anxiety)

- Herb 1: (e.g., chamomile)
- Herb 2: (e.g., lemon balm)

Step 3: Plan How to Incorporate Herbs into Your Daily Routine

Decide how you will use these herbs daily. Consider teas, tinctures, capsules, or adding fresh herbs to your meals. Be consistent and track your progress.

Herb Incorporation Plan

Ginger

- Form: Fresh ginger tea

- How: Boil slices of fresh ginger in water for 10 minutes. Drink 1 cup in the morning.

- Frequency: Daily

Peppermint

- Form: Peppermint tea

- How: Steep 1 teaspoon of dried peppermint leaves in hot water for 5 minutes.

- Frequency: After meals

Tracking Progress

Create a simple log to track your feelings and any improvements you notice. This can help you understand what works best for you.

Progress Log

Date	MMDDYY
Herbs Taken	Ginger
Form	Tea
Dosage	1 cup
Effects	Better digestion
Date	MMDDYY
Herbs Taken	Elderberry
Form	Syrup
Dosage	1 teaspoon
Effects	No cold

By following this template, you can create a personalized herbal remedy plan that aligns with your health goals and fits into your daily life.

Wrapping Up

This chapter taught us about herbs that can cater to your specific needs. We've discussed herbs' solutions for chronic conditions, digestion, and pain relief and how herbs can offer care for children. There are diverse ways to interact with herbs; it's all about finding a way that suits you and your needs. After consulting with your healthcare provider, you can also create a plan of goals and the herbs to use.

Having explored the specialized applications of herbal remedies, it's time to advance our knowledge further. The next chapter delves into advanced herbal preparations, uncovering the secrets to creating more complex and potent herbal formulations.

Chapter 10

DEVELOPING EXPERTISE

Venturing beyond the basics, this chapter opens the door to the artistry of herbal blends, where each combination is a symphony of healing. Here, we explore the advanced realm of herbal remedies, merging ancient wisdom with modern innovation. Here, we'll dig deeper into this herbal world, going beyond to explore the hidden paths.

The Herbal Magic Mix: Crafting Perfect Blends

Ever wonder why some herbal teas knock your socks off while others taste like sad leaves in hot water? Well, it's all about the art of creating complex herbal blends. Imagine being a magical potion master without the creepy cauldron and pointy hat, and let's dive into the fun, fragrant world of herbal synergy and how to create blends that'll make you feel incredible.

Guidelines for Combining Herbs Like a Pro

- **Know your herbs:** First, get to know your herbs' personalities. Some are soothing (like chamomile), while others are invigorating (hello, ginger), and others are just there to add a bit of zing (like peppermint).

- **Balance is key:** Like any great recipe, balance is crucial. Too much of a strong herb can overpower the blend. Aim for harmony where each herb plays its part without hogging the spotlight.

- **Pairing for purpose:** Consider what you want your blend to do. Need to relax? Combine calming herbs like lavender and lemon balm. Looking for a pick-me-up? Mix energizing herbs like ginseng and green tea.

- **Experiment and adjust:** Don't be afraid to play around. Start with tiny amounts, taste test, and tweak as you go. Remember, it's all about finding the perfect mix that works for you.

The Science of Synergy

In the world of herbal blends, 1 + 1 can equal 3. This magic math is called synergy. When certain herbs are combined, they can enhance each other's effects, creating a more powerful result than they would individually. This is why blending isn't just about throwing a bunch of herbs together; it's about creating a team that works better together.

Here are a few examples:

- Chamomile plus valerian root: These two are like the dynamic duo of relaxation. Chamomile is calming, and valerian root is a natural sedative. Together, they can help you relax and get a good night's sleep.

- Peppermint plus ginger: Need a digestive aid? Peppermint soothes your tummy, and ginger helps with nausea and digestion. Together, they're a digestive dynamic duo.

Effective Herbal Blends for Various Conditions

- Stress relief: Mix chamomile, lavender, and lemon balm. This trio will help you unwind and calm your mind.

- Immunity booster: Combine echinacea, elderberry, and astragalus. These herbs are known for their immune-boosting properties.

- Digestive health: Blend fennel, peppermint, and ginger for a soothing digestive tonic.

The Ancient Wisdom of Chinese Medicine

As we continue to explore herb–herb combinations, this concept is nothing new to the Chinese. In fact, according to Che et al. (2013), this practice has been taking place for thousands of years, and it's not just about throwing herbs into a pot; it's a carefully crafted system based on lots of observation and thinking. The following is a simple breakdown of how it works and why it's interesting.

Balancing Act: Yin and Yang and the Five Elements

Chinese medicine is all about balance. Imagine your body is like a delicate scale that needs to stay perfectly level. This balance is based on yin and yang (the balance between day and night) and the five elements (wood, fire, earth, metal, and water). You get sick if something tips the scale too far in one direction—like too much cold or heat. Chinese doctors use herbs, acupuncture, and other fascinating techniques to bring you back into balance.

The Magic of Herbal Blends

Chinese herbalism isn't about using one plant at a time. Instead, it's about mixing several plants (and sometimes animal or mineral substances) to make a potent concoction called a "fu-fang." Here's how it works:

> Through synergy: This is where the herbs work together to make the blend more effective than each herb alone.

> Through positive and negative interactions: When mixing herbs, doctors consider how

they interact. Some herbs help each other out (complementation), while others might clash (antagonism). The goal is to create the best possible blend for treating specific conditions.

Examples of Super Effective Herbal Blends

Decoction of Ephedra (Mahuang-Tang)

Ingredients:

Ephedra, cinnamon twig, bitter apricot seed, and licorice root

Uses:

This blend tackles symptoms like coughing, asthma, headaches, and general aches during a cold. According to Chinese medicine, these symptoms are due to too much "coldness" and "wind" in the body. Each herb in the mix helps balance this, just like modern cold medicines combine ingredients to fight fever, suppress coughs, and clear nasal congestion.

Pulse-Activating Powder (Shengmai San)

Ingredients:

Ginseng root, dwarf lilyturf (*Ophiopogon*) root, and magnolia vine (*Schisandra*) fruit.

Uses:

This blend is a lifesaver for people with a deficiency of qi (energy) and yin (vital fluids). It helps with symptoms like heavy sweating, dry mouth, shortness of breath, thirst, and weak pulse. Ginseng boosts qi, dwarf lilyturf replenishes yin, and magnolia vine strengthens both while stopping excessive sweating. Modern studies suggest it might help with heart conditions like heart failure and viral myocarditis (Che et al., 2013).

The Six Modes of Herbal Interactions

When creating these potent multi-herb concoctions, Chinese medicine follows six main principles to make sure the blend is safe and effective:

- **Reinforcement:** Boosting the effect of an herb

- **Potentiation:** Making an herb's effect stronger

- **Restraint:** Holding back any harmful effects

- **Detoxification:** Neutralizing any toxic parts

- **Counteraction:** Balancing out any negatives with positives

- **Toxicity:** Carefully managing any potential toxic effects

Now, there you have it! Chinese medicine isn't just about treating symptoms; it's about restoring balance and harmony in the body. Although scientific evidence of "their therapeutic benefits is lacking" (Che et al., 2013), we can still achieve amazing health benefits that have stood the test of time.

Herbs for the Long Haul: Mastering Long-Term Regimens for Chronic

Conditions

Committing to something isn't easy to achieve, but it's worth it in the long haul when it comes to our health. In this part of the chapter, we're diving into the world of long-term herbal regimens, especially for those pesky chronic conditions that often trouble seniors. Ready to become an herbal hero? Let's go!

Developing Your Long-Term Herbal Plan

- **Identify your needs:** Start by figuring out what you're dealing with. Common chronic conditions in seniors include arthritis, high blood pressure, diabetes, and digestive issues. Each condition will require a different herbal approach.

- **Choose the right herbs:** Select herbs known to help with your specific condition. Here are a few examples:

  ☐ Arthritis: Turmeric (is anti-inflammatory) and ginger (relieves pain)

  ☐ High blood pressure: Hawthorn (supports heart health) and garlic (lowers blood pressure)

  ☐ Diabetes: Cinnamon (regulates blood sugar) and fenugreek (improves insulin function)

  ☐ Digestive issues: Peppermint (soothes the stomach) and fennel (aids digestion)

- **Create a routine:** Consistency is integral in herbal regimens. Decide on a daily routine that fits your lifestyle. For instance, take your herbs at the same time every day—maybe with breakfast or before bed.

- **Start slowly:** Introduce one herb at a time to see how your body reacts. If something doesn't agree with you, it's easier to pinpoint the culprit.

- **Mix it up:** Long-term use of the same herb can sometimes reduce effectiveness. Rotate different herbs every few months to keep your body responsive.

Effective Use of Herbal Remedies: Tips for Consistency, Tracking, and Safety

Stay consistent: Herbs need time to work their magic. Unlike popping a painkiller, herbal remedies often require weeks or even months to show results. Stick with your regimen, and don't skip doses.

Keep a journal: Track your daily intake and any changes in your symptoms. Note any improvements, side effects, or anything unusual. This helps you and your healthcare provider understand how well the herbs work.

Arrange regular checkups: Stay in touch with your doctor, especially if you're dealing with a serious condition. They can monitor your progress and ensure your herbal regimen is safe and effective. Always let your doctor know about any herbs you're taking to avoid potential interactions with medications.

Adjust as needed: Your body's needs might change over time. Be ready to tweak your regimen based on how you're feeling and any advice from your healthcare provider.

A Simple Example

Let's say you're managing arthritis. Here's a basic long-term herbal regimen:

Morning: Turmeric capsule with breakfast to reduce inflammation

Afternoon: Ginger tea to help with pain relief

Evening: Epsom salt bath with a few drops of lavender oil to relax muscles and joints

Keep a journal to note how your pain levels and mobility improve. Visit your doctor regularly to discuss your progress and any necessary adjustments to your regimen.

By staying consistent and monitoring your progress, you can harness the power of herbs to manage chronic conditions and improve your quality of life. Remember, the journey to better health is a marathon, not a sprint. Stay patient, stay informed, and enjoy the herbal ride!

Herbs in the Modern World: New Innovations and Techniques

In our world, it becomes increasingly important to learn how to adapt. With advancements in technology, it was inevitable that herbal medicine would get a modern makeover. With new advancements and innovative techniques, herbs are stepping up their game. Let's dive into the latest trends and see how technology and research are shaping the future of herbal remedies.

Recent Advancements in Herbal Medicine

- **Standardized extracts:** One of the best innovations in herbal medicine is the creation of standardized extracts. This means that each dose of your herbal supplement has the same amount of active ingredients. No more guessing if you're getting too much or too little—it's all perfectly measured!

- **Herbal supplements in capsules and tablets:** Forget about brewing tea or mixing powders. Nowadays, you can get your herbs in easy-to-swallow capsules and tablets. This makes taking your daily dose super convenient, especially if you're always on the go.

- **Topical applications:** Herbs aren't just for eating or drinking anymore. You can find herbal creams, ointments, and even patches that deliver herbal goodness directly through your skin—great for localized pain relief or skin conditions!

Technology and Research in Herbal Practices

- **Scientific research:** Researchers are now studying herbs more closely than ever. They're conducting clinical trials to understand how herbs work and how effective they are. This means we're getting more reliable information about which herbs to use for specific conditions.

- **Extraction techniques:** Modern technology has improved the extraction of active herb ingredients. Advanced methods like supercritical CO_2 extraction ensure pure, potent extracts without harmful solvents.

- **DNA barcoding:** To avoid any mix-ups or adulteration, scientists use DNA barcoding to identify herbs accurately. This technology ensures that what's on the label is precisely what's in the bottle.

Other Innovations Influencing Modern Herbal Practices

- **Personalized herbal medicine:** Like personalized diets, we now have personalized herbal medicine. By analyzing your genetics and health history, practitioners can create customized herbal formulas for you. It's like having a custom-made herbal regimen!

- **Herb–drug interaction databases:** Knowing how they interact is crucial with more people using herbs and prescription drugs. Online databases now provide detailed information about potential interactions, helping you and your healthcare provider make safer choices.

- **Sustainable sourcing:** As the demand for herbs grows, so does the need for sustainable practices. Many companies now focus on ethically sourced and environmentally friendly harvesting methods, which help protect our planet while providing high-quality herbs.

- **Integrative medicine:** Herbal medicine is increasingly being integrated into mainstream healthcare. Doctors and alternative practitioners work together to combine the best of both worlds, offering more comprehensive care. This approach often involves using herbs alongside conventional treatments for a more balanced and effective therapy.

- **Digital health tools:** Apps and online platforms now help you track your herbal intake, monitor your health, and even get advice from herbal experts. These digital tools make managing your herbal regimen easier and more interactive.

The Future Is Bright for Herbal Medicine

With all these innovations, herbal medicine is more accessible, reliable, and effective than ever. Whether you're a long-time herbal enthusiast or a curious newcomer, the future of herbal remedies looks promising. So why not embrace these modern approaches and see how they can enhance your health and well-being?

Stay curious, stay healthy, and happy herbing!

Herbal Regimen Planning Worksheet

Creating a personalized herbal regimen can be a transformative journey toward optimal health and well-being. Use this worksheet to define your health goals, choose the right herbs, and plan a schedule that works for you. Remember, consistency is key, and it's essential to consult with a healthcare provider before starting any new herbal regimen.

Step 1: Define Your Health Goals

Take a moment to reflect on what you want to achieve with your herbal regimen. Be specific and realistic about your goals.

Step 2: Research and Select Appropriate Herbs

Based on your health goals, research herbs that may support your objectives. Consider their properties, benefits, and any potential side effects or interactions. Below is an example:

> Goal: To improve sleep
>
> Herb: Valerian root
>
> Benefits: Promotes relaxation and improves sleep quality
>
> Potential side effects or interactions: May cause drowsiness; avoid driving after use

Step 3: Outline Your Herbal Regimen Schedule

Determine how and when you will take each herb. Consistency is crucial, so plan a schedule that you can stick to. Below is an example:

> Herb: Valerian root
>
> Dosage: 300 mg
>
> Frequency: Once daily
>
> Time of day: Evening
>
> Note: Take 30 minutes before bedtime

Step 4: Monitor Your Progress

Keep track of how you feel and any changes you notice. Adjust your regimen as needed based on your observations and feedback from your healthcare provider. Take note of your weekly observations and the changes or adjustments needed.

Weekly Progress Journal:

Week 1:

Week 2:

Week 3:

Week 4:

Step 5: Reflect and Revise

Periodically review your goals and progress. Reflect on what's working and what's not, and make necessary adjustments to your regimen.

Reflection Questions:

- Have I achieved any of my health goals? If yes, how did the herbs contribute?

- Are there any herbs I need to replace or adjust the dosage or frequency?

- How do I feel overall since starting this regimen?

Remember, the journey to better health is personal and unique to each individual. Stay patient, be consistent, and, most importantly, listen to your body.

Wrapping Up

During this chapter, we've explored the depths of herb–herb combinations that we can use to bolster our health. Creating the perfect herbal tea blends is an art that can make you feel terrific. Understanding how to mix herbs properly is vital to making delicious and effective herbal teas. It's all about balance, purpose, and a bit of experimentation. Synergy plays a significant role, where combined herbs create more powerful effects. Traditional Chinese medicine has long used these principles to balance the body's energies. Long-term herbal regimens can help manage chronic conditions, and modern advancements are making herbal medicine more accessible and effective.

Key Takeaways

Understanding Herbs

- Know the unique effects of different herbs.

- Balance is crucial for a harmonious blend.

- Match herbs to your desired effect (relaxation, energy, etc.).

Creating Effective Blends

- Combine herbs with complementary effects (e.g., chamomile plus valerian root for relaxation).

- Adjust quantities and experiment to find the perfect mix.

- Identify needs and select appropriate herbs (e.g., turmeric for joint pain).

- Create a consistent routine and monitor progress.

- Adjust as needed based on effectiveness and feedback from healthcare providers.

Modern Innovations in Herbal Medicine

- Standardized extracts: Consistent dosages of active ingredients

- Convenient forms: Capsules, tablets, and topical applications

- Scientific research: Better understanding and validation of herbal effects

- Advanced extraction techniques: Pure and potent extracts

- DNA barcoding: Accurate identification of herbs

Future Trends

- Personalized herbal medicine tailored to individual needs

- Databases for herb–drug interactions

- Sustainable sourcing practices

- Integration of herbal medicine into mainstream healthcare

- Digital health tools for tracking and managing herbal intake

Looking Ahead

With a deeper understanding of advanced herbal preparations, our next step is assembling the essential tools and ingredients. In the upcoming chapter, we'll guide you through building your herbal remedy kit, ensuring you have everything you need to put your newfound knowledge into practice.

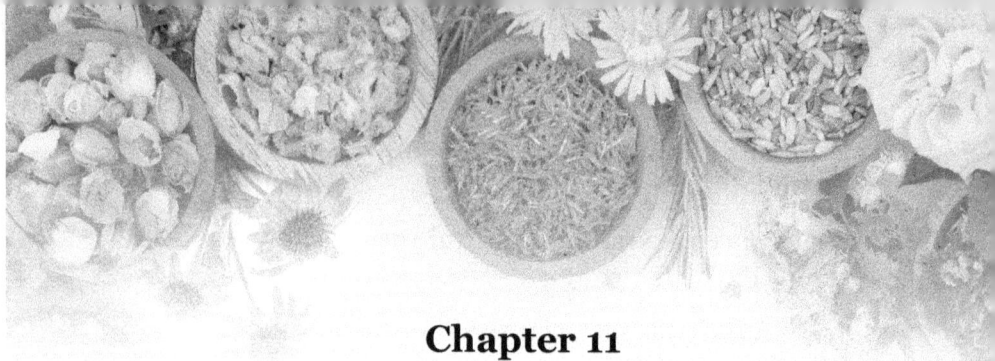

Chapter 11

ESTABLISHING FOUNDATIONS

Imagine having a personalized pharmacy filled with natural, healing herbs at your fingertips. This chapter is your guide to creating a tailored herbal remedy kit that brings the power of nature into your home.

Must-Have Herbs for Every Home Garden

Growing your herbs can be rewarding and practical. Here's a list of essential herbs you can grow in your garden, each with versatile and beneficial uses for various common ailments.

Calendula (Calendula officinalis, Asteraceae)

Uses: The flowers are often used in topical oils and salves to heal wounds, rashes, burns, and dry skin.

Benefits: Calendula is famous for being used in diaper rash ointments. It's excellent for soothing and repairing the skin.

Motherwort (Leonurus cardiaca, Lamiaceae)

Uses: As a tincture or tea, motherwort helps with headaches, menstrual cramps, and muscle pain.

Benefits: Though bitter, it's effective for pain relief, especially in tincture form.

Passionflower (Passiflora incarnata, Passifloraceae)

Uses: The leaves and flowers help promote sleep and alleviate pain such as menstrual cramps and headaches.

Benefits: Passionflower is a calming herb that's easy to grow, particularly if given support like a wall or trellis.

Echinacea (Echinacea purpurea, Asteraceae)

Uses: The roots, seeds, and fresh flowers can be made into an immune-boosting tea or tincture.

Benefits: Echinacea is easy to grow, attracts pollinators, and is drought resistant. It's incredible at stimulating the immune system.

Holy Basil (Ocimum tenuiflorum syn. O. sanctum, Lamiaceae)

Uses: The leaves and flowers are used in teas for colds, coughs, asthma, bronchitis, headaches, arthritis, diabetes, stress, and anxiety.

Benefits: Holy basil is antimicrobial, uplifting, and helps with mental clarity and focus.

Meadowsweet (Filipendula ulmaria, Rosaceae)

Uses: The flowers are used to flavor meads and can be made into herbal syrups for drinks like root beer.

Benefits: Meadowsweet is attractive and adds a pleasant flavor to beverages. It's also good for digestive health.

Jiaogulan (Gynostemma pentaphyllum, Cucurbitaceae)

Uses: The leaves are brewed into a tea for anxiety, stress, depression, high blood pressure, and high cholesterol.

Benefits: Known as southern ginseng, Jiaogu-lan is easy to grow and contains compounds like ginseng, promoting longevity and vitality.

Paracress (Acmella oleracea, Asteraceae)

Uses: The flowers relieve toothaches and are used in oral hygiene products.

Benefits: Paracress is antimicrobial and stimulates saliva production, offering a natural remedy for oral discomfort.

Stinging Nettles (Urtica dioica, Urticaceae)

Uses: The leaves and seeds are used in teas and foods for allergies and arthritis and as a kidney tonic.

Benefits: High in vitamins and minerals, nettles are nutritious and can be added to various dishes once cooked to remove the sting.

Wild Bergamot (Monarda fistulosa, Lamiaceae)

Uses: The leaves and flowers treat infections, digestive issues, and respiratory congestion.

Benefits: Antimicrobial and anti-inflammatory, wild bergamot is also used in steam inhalations to relieve respiratory symptoms.

How to Use These Herbs

Calendula: Infuse the flowers in a carrier oil like olive oil to make an oil or salve. Use this to soothe skin irritations.

Motherwort: To relieve pain, create a tincture by soaking the herb in alcohol or making a strong tea.

Passionflower: Brew tea using the leaves and flowers to help with sleep and pain.

Echinacea: Make tea or tincture from the roots, seeds, or fresh flowers to boost your immune system.

Holy basil: Steep the leaves and flowers in hot water for a tea that aids in respiratory issues and stress.

Meadowsweet: Use the flowers to flavor drinks or make an herbal syrup for digestive health.

Jiaogulan: Brew tea from the leaves to help with stress and improve overall vitality.

Paracress: Chew the flowers or use homemade mouthwash for toothache relief.

Stinging nettles: Add cooked nettles to soups, stews, or brew tea for its nutritional benefits.

Wild bergamot: Use dried leaves and flowers in a steam inhalation to help clear respiratory congestion.

Growing these versatile herbs in your garden allows you to create natural remedies for various common ailments and enhance your home apothecary with fresh, effective ingredients.

Healing: Essential Tools and Resources for Homemade Remedies

Making herbal remedies at home is a fun and rewarding way to take charge of your health. To get started, you'll need some basic tools and resources. Below is a list of essential items and where you can find them.

Ideal Gadgets for Crafting Herbal Magic

Scissors and Baskets

Uses: Scissors are great for harvesting herbs, and baskets are perfect for collecting and drying them.

Where to buy: Garden centers, craft stores, or online at places like Amazon and Etsy

Fine Mesh Sieve

Uses: Sieves (in assorted sizes) are used to strain out herbs from liquids after making teas, infusions, or tinctures.

Where to buy: Kitchen supply stores, department stores, and online retailers like Amazon and Bed Bath & Beyond

Potato Ricer

Uses: A potato ricer can be handy for pressing out the liquid from cooked or soaked herbs.

Where to buy: Most kitchenware stores, department stores, and online shops like Amazon

Mortar and Pestle

Uses: This tool is essential for grinding herbs into powders or pastes.

Where to buy: Kitchen stores, health food stores, and online sites like Amazon and Williams Sonoma

Spice Grinder

Uses: A spice grinder is helpful for finely grinding dried herbs.

Where to buy: Kitchenware stores, big-box retailers like Walmart, and online at Amazon

Kitchen Scale

Uses: A scale is essential for measuring herbs accurately.

Where to buy: Kitchen supply stores, department stores, and online retailers like Amazon and Target

Stainless Steel Funnel

Uses: Funnels help pour liquids into bottles or jars without spilling.

Where to buy: Kitchen supply stores, big-box stores, and online at Amazon

Tea Press

Uses: A tea press makes strong herbal teas or infusions.

Where to buy: Specialty tea shops, kitchen stores, and online retailers like Amazon

Tea Strainer

Uses: Strainers are used to filter out herbs from your brewed tea.

Where to buy: Kitchen stores, tea shops, and online at Amazon

Electric Teapot

Uses: An electric teapot is convenient for quickly boiling water for your teas.

Where to buy: Kitchen supply stores, big-box retailers like Target, and online at Amazon

Suggested Resources for Tools

Amazon: A one-stop shop for almost all the tools listed. You can read reviews and often find good deals

Williams Sonoma: Great for high-quality kitchenware like mortar and pestle and spice grinders

Etsy: Ideal for unique or handmade items like baskets and some specialized tools

Walmart: Convenient for picking up basic kitchen tools at affordable prices

Target: Another good option for kitchen scales, electric teapots, and other kitchen essentials

Specialty tea shops: Best for finding tea presses and strainers designed explicitly for brewing

With these essential tools, you'll be well-equipped to start making your herbal remedies at home. Each tool significantly prepares natural remedies, from harvesting with scissors and baskets to grinding herbs with a mortar and pestle. Check out the suggested resources to find the best tools for your needs and start your journey into homemade herbal medicine.

Harvesting Happiness: My Journey With Herb Gardening and the Joys Along the Way

Growing herbs at home has been one of my life's most satisfying gardening experiences, and let me tell you, it's also surprisingly simple. As beneficial as herbs are for our health, what's often overlooked is the sheer joy that herb gardening brings, even before we harvest them for their wonderful uses. In the world of gardening, herb gardening has its own special magic.

I feel immediately calm when I step outside to tend to my herb garden. There's something profoundly therapeutic about being outdoors, working with the earth. As I plant, weed, and watch the bugs, butterflies, and hummingbirds flutter by, any stress I have seems to melt away. Even if I only have a few minutes to spend with my herbs, those moments of being one with nature are incredibly grounding.

One of my favorite aspects of herb gardening is the delightful scents. When I brush past my mint plants or snip some rosemary, the air fills with their wonderful aroma. It's like a mini aromatherapy session right in my backyard. I can't help but smile every time I catch a whiff. These scents bring joy and a sense of peace. Life can get busy and overwhelming, but my herb garden is my sanctuary. Taking a break from the hustle and bustle of the day to tend to my herbs feels like hitting the reset button. Nurturing these plants, seeing them grow, and smelling their sweet fragrance is deeply fulfilling.

Growing herbs isn't just about the end product but the journey. The simple act of being outside, hands in the soil, and surrounded by the scents and sights of nature brings a unique kind of happiness that's hard to find elsewhere. My herb garden has become a treasured part of my life, offering physical benefits and a profound sense of well-being. I can't recommend it enough if you've ever considered starting your own herb garden, even if it's just a few in containers on a patio or windowsill. It's a small effort with immeasurable rewards.

Growing and Sourcing Your Own Medicinal Herbs: A Simple Guide with a Smile

Whether you're a seasoned green thumb or just starting out, this guide will help you source and grow high-quality herbs at home. Plus, we'll keep it light and fun—because gardening should be a joy, not a chore!

Sourcing High-Quality Herbs

Before you start growing your own, sometimes, it's easier to source herbs from trusted suppliers. Here are some wonderful places to find top-notch herbs, many of which offer discounts for students or bulk purchases:

- Mountain Rose Herbs: Great for a wide variety of herbs, even offering discounts for Herbal Academy students
- Bulk Herb Store: Another excellent source with student discounts
- Jean's Greens: Highly recommended for fresh and dried herbs
- Zack Woods Herb Farm: Student-recommended for quality and service
- Frontier Co-op: Ideal for wholesale purchases
- Rosemary's Garden: Another student favorite
- Healing Spirits Herb Farm: Known for its organic options
- Rebecca's Herbal Apothecary & Supply: Loved by students
- Monterey Bay Spice Company: Great for bulk herbs and spices

(For a complete list, check out the sources mentioned earlier—lots of great options!)

Tips for Growing Your Own Medicinal Herbs

Step 1: Set Your Intentions

First things first—ask yourself why you want to grow an herb garden. Are you doing this for personal use, for your family, or maybe to start a small business? Knowing your goal will help guide your gardening journey.

For personal use: Focus on herbs that you and your family will use regularly.

Small business apothecary: Choose a variety of popular medicinal herbs.

Wholesale: Plan for larger quantities and consider the market demand.

Step 2: Assess Your Space

Consider the space you have available for your garden. Whether using a small balcony or a large backyard, there's always a way to make it work.

Containers: This is perfect for renters or small spaces. Plus, you can move them around!

Garden beds: If you have the space, raised beds are fantastic for growing herbs.

Expandable space: Think about future expansion—will you have room to grow more if you want to?

Step 3: Evaluate Your Energy and Resources

Gardening can be as simple or as involved as you make it. Before diving in, consider your energy levels, time, and resources.

Solo or team effort: Do you fly solo or have helpers? This will affect how much you can manage.

Time commitment: Be realistic about how much time you can dedicate to your garden.

Budget: You don't need much money to start—get creative with the materials you have around the house.

Growing Basics for Seniors

Here are some easy-to-grow herbs that are perfect for beginners and seniors alike:

- Calendula (pot marigold) is great for healing wounds, rashes, and dry skin. Plus, it's the secret ingredient in many diaper rash creams.

- Motherwort is excellent for pain relief. It isn't very pleasant, so a tincture might be better than tea.

- Passionflower helps promote sleep and alleviate pain. This vine loves to climb, so give it a trellis!

- Echinacea (purple coneflower), beautiful and tough, boosts the immune system.

- Holy basil (tulsi) is aromatic and antimicrobial. This herb is a powerhouse for colds, stress, and anxiety.

- Madowsweet has lovely flowers and is excellent for making homemade root beer syrup.

- Jiaogulan (southern ginseng) helps with stress and high cholesterol; brew this for a tonic tea.

- Paracress (toothache plant) numbs toothaches and stimulates saliva; plus, it looks like an eyeball!

- Stinging nettles are nutritious and great in soups or teas. This is commonly found in yards as a "weed."

- Wild bergamot is perfect for treating infections and digestive issues.

Build Your Own Herbal Remedy Kit: A Simple Checklist

Putting together your herbal remedy kit is both fun and practical. Here's a simple checklist to help you get started. This list includes essential herbs, tools, and supplies. Feel free to add your personal favorites and make it your own!

Essential Herbs

- ☐ Calendula (pot marigold)
- ☐ Motherwort
- ☐ Passionflower
- ☐ Echinacea (purple coneflower)
- ☐ Holy basil (tulsi)
- ☐ Meadowsweet
- ☐ Jiaogulan (southern ginseng)
- ☐ Paracress (toothache plant)
- ☐ Wild bergamot

Essential Tools

- ☐ Scissors and baskets
- ☐ Fine mesh sieve (in various sizes)
- ☐ Potato ricer
- ☐ Mortar and pestle
- ☐ Spice grinder
- ☐ Kitchen scale
- ☐ Stainless steel funnel
- ☐ Tea press
- ☐ Tea strainer
- ☐ Electric teapot

Supplies

- ☐ Glass jars (in various sizes)
- ☐ Dropper bottles
- ☐ Labels and marker
- ☐ Cheesecloth

☐ Spray bottles

☐ Small saucepan

☐ Measuring cups and spoons

Print out this checklist and use it as a guide while you build your herbal remedy kit. Happy herb crafting!

Wrapping Up: Final Takeaways

From what we've discussed, it's possible to create a personalized tool kit in numerous ways:

- Know what herbs to have.

- Plant essential herbs.

- Find where to get key resources and tools.

- Ensure you have the essential tools and resources for the garden.

- Set out a clear plan which includes having clear intentions, assessing your space, and evaluating your resources.

- Create a personalized checklist.

Looking Ahead

As we close the final chapter on building your herbal remedy kit, we reflect on our journey together, exploring the ancient wisdom and modern applications of herbal remedies. Let's wrap up this enriching exploration by revisiting the key insights and lessons learned, ensuring you're fully equipped to embrace the world of herbal medicine with confidence and curiosity.

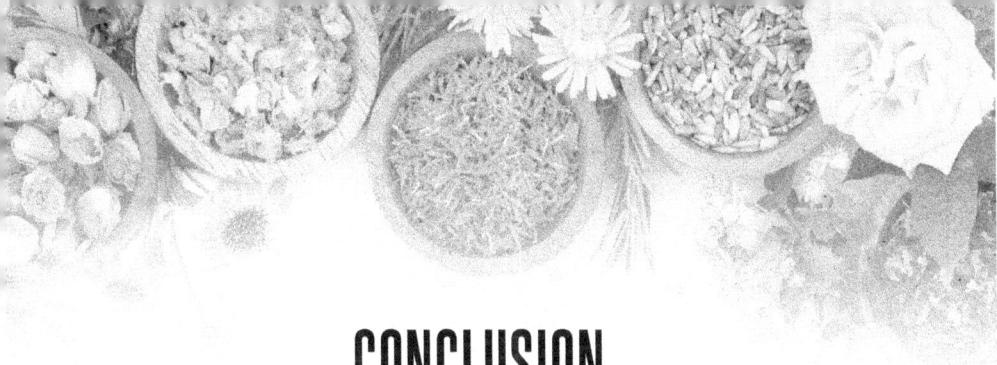

CONCLUSION

We've come to the end of our amazing trip exploring the world of herbs and nature. Together, we've looked back at the history of herbs, learned about their essential parts, and busted some common myths. The most important thing to remember is that herbs can lead to a healthier, happier life. By understanding your health needs, you can use the plants around you to help avoid many health problems. Take this knowledge with confidence and hope for a healthier future. The power of herbs is in your hands.

As we wrap up, remember that this begins a lifelong path to discovery and wellness. You've gained the knowledge to tap into the healing power of nature, which offers both health and balance. Take one herb from your new collection and start using it every day. It could be a calming chamomile tea before bed to help you relax or a peppermint infusion to help with digestion. Try it out and see the benefits for yourself.

In addition, sharing what you've learned with friends and family can be very powerful. Your experience might inspire them to explore herbal remedies, spreading wellness and natural health throughout your community. When people see the positive changes in your life, they might become curious and want to try it themselves. By sharing your knowledge, you can help others start their path toward better health and well-being and become a part of a community that values natural health.

This isn't just the end of a book; it's the start of an ongoing journey. Embrace the principles of the herbal guide as your constant companion on this exciting path to natural health. Herbs are a wonderful resource that can support a healthy lifestyle; now, you have the knowledge to use them effectively. Remember, the journey doesn't stop here. Keep exploring, learning, and growing. There is always more to discover about the incredible benefits of herbs, and the possibilities for your health are endless.

Imagine waking up daily with more energy, feeling more balanced and in tune with your body. Herbs can help make this a reality. Whether using ginger to soothe a sore throat, lavender to help you sleep, or turmeric to reduce inflammation, herbs offer simple and natural ways to improve your health. By making small changes and integrating herbs into your daily routine, you can experience significant improvements in your overall well-being.

Keep a journal of your experiences with different herbs, note what works best for you and your family, and continue to build on your knowledge. The more you learn, the more confident you will become in using herbs to support your health.

As you move forward, remember to listen to your body and pay attention to how it responds to different herbs. Everyone is different, and what works for one person might not work for another. Be patient and open-minded, and give yourself time to find what suits you best.

Lastly, I would love to hear about your experiences and how this book has helped you. Please take a moment to leave a review. Your feedback is valuable and would help others discover the benefits of herbs. It also supports the spread of natural wellness, encouraging more people to live healthier, happier lives.

Thank you for joining me on this journey. Here's to a healthier, more harmonious way of living, with herbs as your trusted allies.

REFERENCES

A forager's checklist for safe, sustainable & ethical foraging. (2022, January 15). Gather and Grow. https://gatherandgrow.com/blog/a-foragers-checklist-for-safe-sustainable-amp-ethical-foraging

Aayushi. (2021, April 19). *These 7 stress-relief herbs will also work against your anxiety.* Healthshots. https://www.healthshots.com/mind/mental-health/these-7-stress-relief-herbs-will-also-work-against-your-anxiety/

Abdullahi, A. A. (2011). Trends and challenges of traditional medicine in Africa. *African Journal of Traditional, Complementary and Alternative Medicines,* *8*(5S). https://doi.org/10.4314/ajtcam.v8i5s.5

Adams, C. (2014). *Herbal medicine.* CreateSpace.

Ahmad Khan, M. S., & Ahmad, I. (2019, January 1). *Chapter 1 - Herbal medicine: Current trends and future prospects.* ScienceDirect. https://www.sciencedirect.com/science/article/abs/pii/B978012814619400001X

Ahmad, I., Aqil, F., Ahmad, F., & Owais, M. (n.d.). Herbal medicines: Prospects and constraints. *Modern phytomedicine,* 59–77. https://doi.org/10.1002/9783527609987.ch3

Alostad, A. H., Steinke, D. T., & Schafheutle, E. I. (2020). Herbal medicine classification: Policy recommendations. *Frontiers in Medicine,* *7.* https://doi.org/10.3389/fmed.2020.00031

Altizer, K. P., Quandt, S. A., Grzywacz, J. G., Bell, R. A., Sandberg, J. C., & Arcury, T. A. (2011). Traditional and commercial herb use in health self-management among rural multiethnic older adults. *Journal of Applied Gerontology, 32*(4), 387–407. https://doi.org/10.1177/0733464811424152

Ananchaisarp, T., Rungruang, S., Theerakulpisut, S., Kamsakul, P., Nilbupha, N., Chansawangphop, N., Yiambunya, J., Jarudamrongsak, J., & Prasertsri, K. (2021). Usage of herbal medicines among the elderly in a primary care unit in Hat Yai, Songkhla province, Thailand. *Asian Biomedicine, 15*(1), 35–42. https://doi.org/10.2478/abm-2020-0005

Arcury, T. A., Grzywacz, J. G., Bell, R. A., Neiberg, R. H., Lang, W., & Quandt, S. A. (2007). Herbal remedy use as health self-management among older adults. *The Journals of Gerontology Series B: Psychological Sciences and Social Sciences, 62*(2), S142–S149. https://doi.org/10.1093/geronb/62.2.s142

Armbrecht, A. (2020). *The business of botanicals: Exploring the healing promise of plant medicines in a global industry.* Chelsea Green Publishing.

Asher, G. N., Corbett, A. H., & Hawke, R. L. (2017). Common herbal dietary supplement–Drug interactions. *American Family Physician, 96*(2), 101–107. https://www.aafp.org/pubs/afp/issues/2017/0715/p101.html

Azadnia, R., Al-Amidi, M. M., Mohammadi, H., Cifci, M. A., Daryab, A., & Cavallo, E. (2022). An AI based approach for medicinal plant identification using deep CNN based on global average pooling. *Agronomy, 12*(11), 2723. https://doi.org/10.3390/agronomy12112723

Baker, P. (2023, December 21). *Best plant identification apps for mobile in 2023, tested*

by our editors. CNN Underscored. https://
edition.cnn.com/cnn-underscored/reviews/
best-plant-identification-app

Balekundri, A., & Mannur, V. (2020). Quality control
of the traditional herbs and herbal products: A
review. *Future Journal of Pharmaceutical Sciences,
6*(1). https://doi.org/10.1186/s43094-020-00091-5

Bardia, A., Nisly, N. L., Zimmerman, M. B., Gryzlak,
B. M., & Wallace, R. B. (2007). Use of herbs among
adults based on evidence-based indications:
Findings from the National Health Interview
Survey. *Mayo Clinic Proceedings. Mayo Clinic, 82*(5),
561–566. https://www.ncbi.nlm.nih.gov/pmc/
articles/PMC1964882/

Bauer, B. (2024, March 27). *Herbal treatment for
anxiety: Is it effective?* Mayo Clinic. https://
www.mayoclinic.org/diseases-conditions/
generalized-anxiety-disorder/expert-answers/
herbal-treatment-for-anxiety/faq-20057945

Bedosky, L. (2022, December 1). *7 Herbs and spices for
immune support*. Everyday Health. https://www.
everydayhealth.com/diet-nutrition/herbs-and-
spices-that-may-help-boost-immunity-naturally/

Bhat, M. D. A., & Malik, R. (2022). Challenges in
monitoring the safety of herbal medicines-An
appraisal. *Journal of Pharmacovigilance and Drug
Research, 3*(4), 3–8. https://doi.org/10.53411/
jpadr.2022.3.4.2

Blankespoor, J. (2023a, June 9). *Preparing medicinal
teas*. Chestnut School of Herbal Medicine.
https://chestnutherbs.com/herbal-infusions-and-
decoctions-preparing-medicinal-teas/

Blankespoor, J. (2023b, November 14). *Guidelines to
growing medicinal herbs from seed*. Chestnut School

of Herbal Medicine. https://chestnutherbs.com/
guideline-to-growing-medicinal-herbs-from-seeds/

Blankespoor, J., & Gemma, M. (2014, March 7). *10 Medicinal herbs for the garden*. Chestnut School of Herbal Medicine. https://chestnutherbs.com/ the-top-ten-medicinal-herbs-for-the-garden/

Bloom, L., & Bloom, C. (2016). *Happily ever after...and 39 other myths about love*. New World Library.

Borse, S. P., Singh, D. P., & Nivsarkar, M. (2019). Understanding the relevance of herb–drug interaction studies with special focus on interplays. *Porto Biomedical Journal, 4*(2), e15. https://doi. org/10.1016/j.pbj.0000000000000015

Boye, K. (2023, September 21). *7 Benefits of journaling for mental & physical health*. Gaia Herbs. https:// www.gaiaherbs.com/blogs/seeds-of-knowledge/ journaling-benefits

Brief history herbal medicine. (2018, August 10). Herbal Clinic Swansea. https://www.herbalclinic-swansea. co.uk/herbal-medicine/a-brief-history-of-herbal-medicine/

Bryon, C. (2021, July 2). *10 surprising uses for herbs*. Alive. https://www.alive.com/ lifestyle/10-surprising-uses-for-herbs/

Bumming, M., Woo, D., & Kendall, P. (2014, October). *Herbs: Preserving and using - 9.335*. Colorado State University Extension. https://extension.colostate. edu/topic-areas/nutrition-food-safety-health/ herbs-preserving-and-using-9-335/

Chamomile's calming properties may be real. (2015, March 22). The Detroit News. https://www. detroitnews.com/story/life/food/2015/03/22/ chamomile-tea-health-benefits/25082701/

Charbonneau, J. (2022, October 25). *5 unusual medicinal herbs*. Southern Exposure Seed

Exchange. https://blog.southernexposure.com/2022/10/5-unusual-medicinal-herbs/

Che, C. T., Wang, Z., Chow, M., & Lam, C. (2013). Herb-herb combination for therapeutic enhancement and advancement: Theory, practice and future perspectives. *Molecules, 18*(5), 5125–5141. https://doi.org/10.3390/molecules18055125

Cherney, K. (n.d.). *9 Herbs to fight arthritis pain: Aloe vera, ginger, and more.* Healthline. https://www.healthline.com/health/osteoarthritis/herbs-arthritis-pain

Chevallier, A. (2016). *Encyclopedia of herbal medicine.* Penguin.

Children's dosage guide. (n.d.). Herb Lore. https://herblore.com/overviews/childrens-dosage-guide

Chinese herbal medicine. (2012). Better Health Channel. https://www.betterhealth.vic.gov.au/health/conditionsandtreatments/chinese-herbal-medicine

Choosing a herb supplier for your business. (2021, April 29). KPC. https://kpc.com/articles/why-choosing-a-reliable-herb-supplier-could-benefit-your-business/

Clark, C. (2022, September 8). *17 Best herbalist tools.* ZYTO. https://zyto.com/17-best-herbalist-tools

Classifying herbal medicines. (n.d.). Access2Markets. https://trade.ec.europa.eu/access-to-markets/en/content/classifying-herbal-medicines

Codekas, C. (n.d.). *Herbal bath and skincare recipes.* Grow Forage Cook Ferment. https://www.growforagecookferment.com/herbalism/herbal-bath-skincare-recipes/

Curtis, L. (2022, November 1). *10 Healing herbs with medicine benefits.* Verywell Health. https://www.verywellhealth.com/healing-herbs-5180997

Dana. (2019, September 5). *10 Essential tools every herbalist needs*. Rustic Farm Life. https://www.rusticfarmlife.com/ essential-tools-every-herbalist-needs/

Davis, A. (2023, July 13). *10 Best herbs to start your home herbal apothecary*. Chestnut School of Herbal Medicine. https://chestnutherbs.com/10-best-herbs-to-start-your-home-herbal-apothecary/

Davis, H. (2023, July 7). *Are herbs good for stress?* Nutrisense. https://www.nutrisense.io/blog/ best-herbs-for-stress

De Smet, P. A. G. M. (1995). Health risks of herbal remedies. *Drug Safety*, *13*(2), 81–93. https://doi. org/10.2165/00002018-199513020-00003

De, L. (2015, July 2). *Herbal supplements: Myths smoked*. Nature. https://www.nature. com/scitable/blog/why-science-matters/ herbal_supplements_myths_smoked/

Determining dosages in children. (n.d.). FX Medicine. https://www.fxmedicine.com.au/blog-post/ determining-dosages-children

Dharmananda, S. (n.d.). *Dosage and form of herbs*. ITM Online. http://www.itmonline.org/arts/dosage.htm

Ding, R., Luo, J., Wang, C., Yu, L., Yang, J., Wang, M., Zhong, S., & Gu, R. (2023). Identifying and mapping individual medicinal plant Lamiophlomis rotata at high elevations by using unmanned aerial vehicles and deep learning. *Plant Methods*, *19*(1). https://doi.org/10.1186/ s13007-023-01015-z

Dosing guidelines. (n.d.). Evergreen. https://www. evherbs.com/dosing-guideline

Dragani, M. (2021, January 23). *8 Ways to incorporate turmeric into your wellness routine*. L'Officiel USA. https://www.lofficielusa.com/wellness/8-ways-to-incorporate-turmeric-into-wellness-routine-health-benefits

Du, Y., Wolf, I.-K., Zhuang, W., Bodemann, S., Knöss, W., & Knopf, H. (2014). Use of herbal medicinal products among children and adolescents in Germany. *BMC Complementary and Alternative Medicine*, *14*(1). https://doi.org/10.1186/1472-6882-14-218

Duke, J. A. (2002). *Handbook of medicinal herbs*. CRC Press. https://repository.poltekkes-kaltim.ac.id/1148/1/Handbook%20of%20Medicinal%20Herbs%20(%20PDFDrive%20).pdf

Dwiwijaya, K. A, Suriani, N., Rochmawati, D. R., & Putri, F. S. (2023). Identification of herbal plants using morphology method and k-nearest neighbour algorithm (KNN). *IOP Conference Series: Earth and Environmental Science, 1157(1)*, 012041–012041. https://doi.org/10.1088/1755-1315/1157/1/012041

8 Herbs for hormone balance. (2023, January 10). Feminade. https://feminade.com/blogs/nutrition-supplements/herbs-for-hormone-balance

8 Unusual herbs to grow. (n.d.). PRO-MIX Gardening. https://www.promixgardening.com/en-us/tips/8-unusual-herbs-to-grow-22

Ekor, M. (2014). The growing use of herbal medicines: Issues relating to adverse reactions and challenges in monitoring safety. *Frontiers in Pharmacology*, *4*(177). https://doi.org/10.3389/fphar.2013.00177

El-Dahiyat, F., Rashrash, M., Abuhamdah, S., Abu Farha, R., & Babar, Z.-U.-D. (2020). Herbal medicines: A cross-sectional study to evaluate the prevalence and predictors of use among Jordanian adults. *Journal of Pharmaceutical Policy and Practice*, *13*(1). https://doi.org/10.1186/s40545-019-0200-3

Elderot, S. (n.d.). *Simone Elderot on LinkedIn: Growing herbs is something that I highly recommend to anyone, even if you....* Www.linkedin.com. Retrieved May 31, 2024, from https://www.linkedin.com/posts/simoneelderot_growing-herbs-is-something-that-i-highly-activity-7042515065765261312-Sthh/

11 Herbs you need to know for immune support. (2022, April 4). Gaia Herbs. https://www.gaiaherbs.com/blogs/seeds-of-knowledge/11-herbs-you-need-to-know-for-immune-support

Ewumi, O. (2022, October 6). *Herbal medicine: Types, uses, and safety.* Medical News Today. https://www.medicalnewstoday.com/articles/herbal-medicine#how-to-take-supplements

Explore the 12 best herbs for digestion. (2022, December 19). Organic India. https://organicindiausa.com/blog/herbs-for-digestion/

15 Healthy ways to use fresh mint. (2022, March 19). Elizabeth Rider. https://www.elizabethrider.com/10-ways-use-fresh-mint/

15+ Best female hormone balance herbs. (2023, July 18). Happy Healthy Hippie. https://happyhealthyhippieco.com/blogs/news/hormone-balance-herbs

5 Herbs to supercharge your immune system. (2023, April 5). College of Naturopathic Medicine. https://www.naturopathy-uk.com/news/blog/2023/04/05/5-herbs-to-supercharge-your-immune-system/

5 Myths about popular natural products marketed for disease prevention and wellness. (n.d.). NCCIH. https://www.nccih.nih.gov/health/tips/myths-about-popular-natural-products-marketed-for-disease-prevention-and-wellness

Fletcher, J. (2023, November 22). *Herbal tinctures: 6 Types and recipes*. Medical News Today. https://www.medicalnewstoday.com/articles/324149

Fong, H. H. S. (2002). Integration of herbal medicine into modern medical practices: Issues and prospects. *Integrative cancer therapies, 1*(3), 287–293. https://doi.org/10.1177/153473540200100313

Gardiner, P., & Kemper, K. J. (2000). Herbs in pediatric and adolescent medicine. *Pediatrics in review, 21*(2), 44–57. https://doi.org/10.1542/pir.21-2-44

Geerts, J. (2023, June 9). *3 Ways to preserve medicinal herbs*. Serenity Hill Farmstead. https://serenityhillfarmstead.com/3-ways-to-preserve-medicinal-herbs/

Gelman, L., & David, L. (2022, November 14). *16 Medicinal herbs you can grow*. The Healthy. https://www.thehealthy.com/home-remedies/medicinal-herbs/

Gemma, M., & Blankespoor, J. (2019, January 3). *5 Tonic herbs to boost immunity this winter*. Chestnut School of Herbal Medicine. https://chestnutherbs.com/5-tonic-herbs-to-boost-immunity-this-winter/

Ghosh, N, Ghosh, R, Mandal, V, & Mandal, S. C. (2011). Recent advances in herbal medicine for treatment of liver diseases. *Pharmaceutical Biology, 49*(9), 970–988. https://doi.org/10.3109/13880209.2011.558515

Green Jeeva. (n.d.). *Sourcing traditional medicinal herbs: Overcoming challenges for holistic wellness products*. https://www.greenjeeva.com/blog/sourcing-traditional-medicinal-herbs

Green, J. (2000). *The herbal medicine-maker's handbook*. Crossing Press.

Gregory, J., Vengalasetti, Y. V., Bredesen, D. E., & Rao, R. V. (2021). Neuroprotective herbs for the management of Alzheimer's disease. *Biomolecules*, *11*(4), 543. https://doi.org/10.3390/biom11040543

Harder, C. F. (2020, July 21). *Medicinal herb gardening for beginners*. Chestnut School of Herbal Medicine. https://chestnutherbs.com/medicinal-herb-gardening-for-beginners/

Harold, L. (2023, January 3). *Aromatherapy scents for stress relief*. Verywell Mind. https://www.verywellmind.com/aromatherapy-scents-for-stress-relief-3144599

Harvard Health Publications. (2004, January 22). Buyer's guide to herbs and supplements. Newswise. https://www.newswise.com/articles/buyers-guide-to-herbs-and-supplements

Harvard Health Publishing. (2021, October 21). *The health benefits of 3 herbal teas*. Harvard Health. https://www.health.harvard.edu/nutrition/the-health-benefits-of-3-herbal-teas

Healthcare Business Today. (2021, December 8). *7 Surprising facts about herbs you never knew before*. https://www.healthcarebusinesstoday.com/7-surprising-facts-about-herbs-you-never-knew-before/

Herbal dosage guidelines for children. (n.d.). The Herbal Toad. https://theherbaltoad.com/blog/herbal-dosage-guidelines-for-children/

Herbal first aid checklist. (n.d.). Etsy. https://www.etsy.com/market/herbal_first_aid_checklist?ref=lp_queries_external_bottom-13

Herbal history. (n.d.). Herbal Academy. https://theherbalacademy.com/herbal-history/

Herbal medicine - Innovations (n.d.). International Journal of Innovative Research in Science,

Engineering and Technology. https://www.
iomcworld.org/medical-journals/herbal-medicine--
innovations-49530.html

*Herbal medicine | Complementary and alternative
therapy.* (n.d.). Cancer Research UK. https://
www.cancerresearchuk.org/about-cancer/
treatment/complementary-alternative-therapies/
individual-therapies/herbal-medicine

Herbal medicine information. (n.d.). Mount Sinai Health
System. https://www.mountsinai.org/health-library/
treatment/herbal-medicine

Herbal medicine plants approved by the DOH. (n.d.).
RNpedia. https://www.rnpedia.com/nursing-
notes/community-health-nursing-notes/
herbal-medicine-plants-approved-doh/

Herbal medicine sample business plan. (n.d.). Scribd.
https://www.scribd.com/doc/76669638/
Herbal-Medicine-Sample-Business-Plan

Herbal remedies and complementary medicines.
(2015, April). Royal College of Psychiatrists.
https://www.rcpsych.ac.uk/mental-
health/treatments-and-wellbeing/
complementary-and-alternative-medicines

Herbal tea. (n.d.). Farmhouse Teas. https://www.
farmhouseteas.com/collections/herbal-tea

Herbal tinctures. (n.d.). Birch Botanicals. https://www.
birchbarkbotanicals.com/herbal-tinctures

Herbalist tools. (n.d.). Etsy. https://www.etsy.com/market/
herbalist_tools

Herb-drug interactions. (2021, July). NCCIH. https://
www.nccih.nih.gov/health/providers/digest/
herb-drug-interactions

Herbs - An overview. (n.d.). ScienceDirect.
https://www.sciencedirect.com/topics/
agricultural-and-biological-sciences/herbs

Hill, A. (2020, February 3). *9 Popular herbal medicines: Benefits and uses.* Healthline. https://www.healthline.com/nutrition/herbal-medicine#3.-Ginkgo-biloba

Hobbs, C. (2014, August 12). *History of Western herbalism.* Christopher Hobbs. https://christopherhobbs.com/library/featured-articles/history-of-western-herbalism/

Hobbs, H. (2024, May 7). *Chamomile tea for acid reflux: What you should know.* Healthline. https://www.healthline.com/health/digestive-health/chamomile-tea-acid-reflux

Hoffmaster, D. (2018, July 16). *Creative uses for lemon balm when it takes over your garden!* Turning the Clock Back. https://www.turningclockback.com/creative-uses-for-lemon-balm/

Hoffmaster, D. (2023, June 22). *How to make your own herbal teas.* Treehugger. https://www.treehugger.com/how-to-make-your-own-herbal-tea-recipes-and-instructions-5194393

Hoover, D. D. (2022, June 30). *4 Potential disadvantages of herbal medicine.* SOHMA Integrative Medicine. https://www.sohma.org/herbs/4-potential-disadvantages-of-herbal-medicine/

Hoshaw, C. (2021, May 14). *Herbal medicine 101: How you can harness the power of herbs.* Healthline. https://www.healthline.com/health/herbal-medicine-101-harness-the-power-of-healing-herbs#herbal-products

How to identify plants in the field. (n.d.). American Museum of Natural History. https://www.amnh.org/learn-teach/curriculum-collections/biodiversity-counts/plant-identification/how-to-identify-plants-in-the-field

Indrayanto, G. (2018). Recent development of quality control methods for herbal derived drug preparations. *Natural Product Communications, 13*(12), 1934578X1801301. https://doi.org/10.1177/1934578x1801301208

Irene. (2019, August 23). *How to make herbal salves.* Mountain Rose Herbs. https://blog.mountainroseherbs.com/diy-herbal-salves

James, M. (2013, October 8). *Herbs for digestion.* Women's Health Network. https://www.womenshealthnetwork.com/digestive-health/herbal-remedies-for-digestive-system/

Jamie. (2019, January 9). *How to safely dose herbal remedies for the best results.* The Herbal Spoon. https://www.theherbalspoon.com/dose-herbal-remedies/

Jamshidi-Kia, F., Lorigooini, Z., & Amini-Khoei, H. (2018). Medicinal plants: past history and future perspective. *Journal of Herbmed Pharmacology, 7*(1), 1–7. https://doi.org/10.15171/jhp.2018.01

Johns Hopkins Medicine. (2019). *Chinese medicine.* https://www.hopkinsmedicine.org/health/wellness-and-prevention/chinese-medicine

Jones, T. (2017). *10 Healthy herbal teas you should try.* Healthline. https://www.healthline.com/nutrition/10-herbal-teas

Justis, A. (2015, September 3). *Choosing safe herbs for your kids.* Herbal Academy. https://theherbalacademy.com/choosing-safe-herbs-for-your-kids/

Kent-Stoll, G. (2022, December 23). *Herbal wellness routines on the go for travel and a busy schedule.* Herbal Academy. https://theherbalacademy.com/herbal-wellness-routines/

Khan, M., Ahmed, M., Zafar, M., & Sultana, S. (2007). Treatment of common ailments by plant-based remedies among the people of district Attock (Punjab) of Northern Pakistan. *African Journal of Traditional, Complementary and Alternative Medicines, 4*(1). https://doi.org/10.4314/ajtcam.v4i1.31201

Kiyohara, H., Matsumoto, T., & Yamada, H. (2004). Combination effects of herbs in a multi-herbal formula: Expression of Juzen-taiho-to's immuno-modulatory activity on the intestinal immune system. *Evidence-Based Complementary and Alternative Medicine, 1*(1), 83–91. https://doi.org/10.1093/ecam/neh004

Koithan, M., & Farrell, C. (2010). Indigenous Native American healing traditions. *The Journal for Nurse Practitioners, 6*(6), 477–478. https://doi.org/10.1016/j.nurpra.2010.03.016

Kolen, R. (2017, June 13). *How to make herbal tinctures.* Mountain Rose Herbs. https://blog.mountainroseherbs.com/guide-tinctures-extracts

Kothari, V. (2020). Validation of traditional medicinal practices through modern scientific Approach: A case for reconsideration. *Current Pharmacogenomics and Personalized Medicine, 17*(1), 11–13. https://doi.org/10.2174/1875692118666191223155350

Kubala, J. (2024, June 9). *The 12 best herbs and spices for better health.* Health. https://www.health.com/herbs-and-spices-for-better-health-7480182

La Forge, T. (2021, December 10). *5 Calming herbs and spices to fight stress and anxiety.* Healthline. https://www.healthline.com/health/mental-health/herbs-for-stress-recipe

Lobermeier, K. (2023, August 17). *Preserving freshness: How to hang dry herbs | Step-by-step guide.* Under a Tin Roof. https://underatinroof.com/blog/old-fashioned-preservation-methods-hang-drying-herbs

Lopez-Alt, J. K. (2024, January 18). *The best way to store fresh herbs*. Serious Eats. https://www.seriouseats.com/the-best-way-to-store-fresh-herbs-parsley-cilantro-dill-basil

Macfarlane, S. (2023, October 18). *9 Herbs you need to try for hormone balance*. Wild Dispensary. https://wilddispensary.co.nz/blogs/news/herbs-for-hormone-balance

Mahomoodally, M. F. (2013). Traditional medicines in Africa: An appraisal of ten potent African medicinal plants. *Evidence-Based Complementary and Alternative Medicine, 2013* (617459), 1–14. https://doi.org/10.1155/2013/617459

Malik, O. A, Ismail, N, Hussein, B. R, & Yahya, U. (2022). Automated real-time identification of medicinal plants species in natural environment using deep learning models—A case study from Borneo Region. *Plants, 11*(15), 1952. https://doi.org/10.3390/plants11151952

Manohar, Pr. (2012). Sustainable harvesting of medicinal plants: Some thoughts in search for solutions. *Ancient Science of Life, 32*(1), 1. https://doi.org/10.4103/0257-7941.113789

Mason. (n.d.). *Must-have tools for herbalists*. Mountain Rose Herbs. https://blog.mountainroseherbs.com/tools-for-herbalists

Masterclaa. (2022). *How to identify a plant in 10 steps*. https://extension.psu.edu/plant-identification-preparing-samples-and-using-keys.

McDermott, A. (2018, June 15). *19 Herbs for hair growth*. Healthline. https://www.healthline.com/health/herbs-for-hair-growth

McKenna, D. (n.d.). *Is there good scientific evidence?* The University of Minnesota. https://www. takingcharge.csh.umn.edu/there-good-scientific- evidence#:~:text=Clinical%20studies%20 indicate%20that%20botanical

Mehrabi, D. (2020, February 12). *12 Best herbal skincare products to add to your regimen in 2022.* BHSkin Dermatology. https://bhskin.com/blog/12-best- herbal-skincare-products-2022/mh123. (2022, June 15). *Busting the common myths about herbal medicine.* College of Medicine and Healing Arts. https://comha.org.uk/busting-the-common-myths- about-herbal-medicine/

Mishra, P, Kumar, A, Nagireddy, A, Mani, D. N, Shukla, A. K, Tiwari, R, & Sundaresan, V. (2015). DNA barcoding: An efficient tool to overcome authentication challenges in the herbal market. *Plant Biotechnology Journal, 14*(1), 8–21. https://doi. org/10.1111/pbi.12419

Moreira, D. de L, Teixeira, S. S, Monteiro, M. H. D, De-Oliveira, A. C. A. X, & Paumgartten, F. J. R. (2014). Traditional use and safety of herbal medicines. *Revista Brasileira de Farmacognosia*, *24*(2), 248–257. https://doi.org/10.1016/j.bjp.2014.03.006

Mortlock, S. (2022, September 5). *Mystery and medicine of Native Americans.* The Biomedical Scientist. https://thebiomedicalscientist.net/science/ mystery-and-medicine-native-americans

Motaghi, H. (2022, January 20). *7 Healing herbs for healthy skin and body.* Touch To Heal Spa. https://touchtohealspa. com/7-healing-herbs-for-healthy-skin-and-body/

Mr. X x. (2020). *Herbal medicine quiz.* Quizizz. https://quizizz.com/admin/ quiz/5f094fe42b0944001b6b6aa1/ herbal-medicine-quiz

Muyumba, N. W, Mutombo, S. C, Sheridan, H, Nachtergael, A, & Duez, P. (2021). Quality control of herbal drugs and preparations: The methods of analysis, their relevance and applications. *Talanta Open*, 100070. https://doi.org/10.1016/j.talo.2021.100070

Myth or fact quiz. (n.d.). See the Possibilities. https://www.seethepossibilities.ca/myth-or-fact-quiz/

Natural product testing services. (n.d.). Eurofins Scientific. https://www.eurofinsus.com/food-testing/industries/botanicals/

Nicole. (2016, June 14). *Common herbs, uncommon uses*. Smile Herb School. https://smileherbschool.com/common-herbs-uncommon-uses

NIH. (2022, October 24). *List of herbs in the NLM herb garden*. https://www.nlm.nih.gov/about/herbgarden/list.html

Ongkar, E. (2017, December 17). *7 Creative ways to use peppermint essential oil*. Mountain Rose Herbs. https://blog.mountainroseherbs.com/ways-to-use-peppermint-essential-oil

Online herbal medicine making course. (2018, December 19). Chestnut School of Herbal Medicine. https://chestnutherbs.com/online-herbal-classes/herbal-medicine-making-course/

Pelkonen, O., Xu, Q., & Fan, T.-P. (2014). Why is research on herbal medicinal products important and how can we improve its quality? *Journal of Traditional and Complementary Medicine*, 4(1), 1–7. https://doi.org/10.4103/2225-4110.124323

Petrovska, B. B. (2012). Historical review of medicinal plants' usage. *Pharmacognosy Reviews*, 6(11), 1. https://doi.org/10.4103/0973-7847.95849

Phair, M. (2021). The ancient use of herbal medicine. *American Journal of Ethnomedicine*, *8*(8). https://doi.org/10.36648/2348-9502.21.8.001

Philippine Institute of Traditional and Alternative Health Care. (n.d.). *Directory of Herbs*. https://pitahc.gov.ph/directory-of-herbs/

Place, S. (2022, October 4). *40 Fun ways to use an interactive timeline in your lessons*. BookWidgets. https://www.bookwidgets.com/blog/2022/10/40-fun-ways-to-use-an-interactive-timeline-in-your-lessons

Plant identification: examining leaves. (n.d.). Oregon State University. https://landscapeplants.oregonstate.edu/plant-identification-examining-leaves

Plant identification: Preparing samples and using keys. (2023, March 27). PennState Extension. https://extension.psu.edu/plant-identification-preparing-samples-and-using-keys

Powers, D. (2023, September 26). *The 5 best online herb suppliers*. The Botanical Institute. https://botanicalinstitute.org/best-herb-suppliers/

Rajak, H. (2023, July 14). *Classification of herbs*. hmhub. https://hmhub.in/classification-of-herbs/

Richards, L. (2020, April 3). *Herbs for anxiety: 9 Calming options*. Medical News Today. https://www.medicalnewstoday.com/articles/herbs-for-anxiety

Richmond Natural Medicine. (2018, August 21). *6 Ways to incorporate medicinal herbs into your daily routine*. https://richmondnaturalmed.com/medicinal-herbs-daily-routine/

Rojas, P, Jung-Cook, H, Ruiz-Sánchez, E, Rojas-Tomé, I. S, Rojas, C, López-Ramírez, A. M., & Reséndiz-Albor, A. A. (2022). Historical aspects of herbal use and comparison of current regulations of herbal products between Mexico, Canada and the

United States of America. *International Journal of Environmental Research and Public Health*, *19*(23), 15690. https://doi.org/10.3390/ijerph192315690

Ruggeri, C. (2024, May 3). *Best 101 herbs and spices for healing*. Dr. Axe. https://draxe.com/nutrition/top-herbs-spices-healing/

Safety and toxicity profiling of herbal drugs. (n.d.). Frontiers. https://www.frontiersin.org/research-topics/40643/safety-and-toxicity-profiling-of-herbal-drugs

Sah, A., Naseef, P. P., Kuruniyan, M.S., Jain, G.K., Zakir, F., & Aggarwal, G. (2022). A comprehensive study of therapeutic applications of chamomile. *Pharmaceuticals*, *15*(10), 1284. https://doi.org/10.3390/ph15101284

Salve making: Tips and tricks. (2020, October 1). Prairie Star Botanicals. https://prairiestarbotanicals.com/blogs/news/salve-making-tips-and-tricks

Schrock, K. (2010, May 31). *The hidden health power of spices and herbs is revealed in recent studies*. Scientific American. https://blogs.scientificamerican.com/observations/the-hidden-health-power-of-spices-and-herbs-is-revealed-in-recent-studies/

Senevirathne, L. P. D. S., Pathirana, D. P. D. S., Silva, A. L. Dissanayaka, M. G. S. R., Nawinna, D. P., & Ganegoda, D. (2020). Mobile-based assistive tool to identify and learn medicinal herbs. IEEE. https://doi.org/10.1109/icac51239.2020.9357247

7 Best herbs for female hormone balance. (2018, July 30). Reset Lab. https://resetlab.co.nz/blog/7-best-herbs-for-female-hormone-balance/

7 Creative ways to use rosemary outside of cooking. (2021, August 11). The Optimist Daily. https://www.optimistdaily.com/2021/08/7-creative-ways-to-use-rosemary-outside-of-cooking/

Shahmiri, L., Wong, P., & Dooley, L. S. (2022). *Accurate medicinal plant identification in natural environments by embedding mutual information in a convolution neural network model*. IEEE. https://doi.org/10.1109/ipas55744.2022.10053008

Shane-McWhorter, L. (2009). *American Diabetes Association guide to herbs and nutritional supplements*. American Diabetes Association.

Shanmugam H., Pranav P., & Doble, M. (2022). *Future prospects on synergistic herb-drug interactions*. Springer. https://doi.org/10.1007/978-981-19-5125-1_18

Sharma, A, Sabharwal, P, & Dada, R. (2021, January 1). *Chapter 1 - Herbal medicine—An introduction to its history*. ScienceDirect. https://www.sciencedirect.com/science/article/abs/pii/B9780128155653000011

Shaw, D., Graeme, L, Pierre, D, Elizabeth, W, & Kelvin, C. (2012). Pharmacovigilance of herbal medicine. *Journal of Ethnopharmacology, 140*(3), 513–518. https://doi.org/10.1016/j.jep.2012.01.051

Shawn. (2022, August 16). *Ethical issues in the herb industry: Wildharvesting vs. cultivation*. Mountain Rose Herbs. https://blog.mountainroseherbs.com/ethical-issues-in-the-herb-industry-wildharvesting-vs.-cultivation

Shiffler, A. (2020, June 16). *15 Rare herbs you should consider growing in your garden*. Herbs at Home. https://herbsathome.co/15-rare-herbs-to-grow-in-your-garden/

Simon, N. (2022, June 15). *10 Fresh herbs that have surprising health benefits*. AARP. https://www.aarp.org/health/healthy-living/info-2022/fresh-herb-health-benefits.html

6 Natural health remedies you can try today. (2016, September 2). MetLife. https://www.metlife.com/blog/wellness/holistic-medicine/

6 Tips: How herbs can interact with medicines. (n.d.). NCCIH. https://www.nccih.nih.gov/health/tips/tips-how-herbs-can-interact-with-medicines

Smith, E. B. (2023, May 11). *News you can use: Dispelling myths about natural remedies.* Ole Miss News. https://news.olemiss.edu/news-you-can-use-dispelling-myths-about-natural-remedies/

Soloway, R. A. (n.d.). *Mixing meds, herbs and supplements.* Poison Control. https://www.poison.org/articles/mixing-meds-herbs-and-supplements

Stoller, J. K., Nielsen, C., Buccola, J., & Brateanu, A. (2014). *The Cleveland Clinic Foundation intensive review of internal medicine.* Lippincott Williams & Wilkins

Suharjito, D., Darusman, L. K., Darusman, D., & Suwarno, E. (2014). Comparing medicinal plants use for traditional and modren herbal medicine in Long Nah village of East Kalimantan. *Bionatura-Jurnal Ilmu-ilmu Hayati dan Fisik. 16*(2), 95–102. https://jurnal.unpad.ac.id/bionatura/article/viewFile/7570/3467

Sukovieff, J. (n.d.). *Guidelines for choosing herbal products.* GI Society. https://badgut.org/information-centre/a-z-digestive-topics/guidelines-for-choosing-herbal-products

Surreyfarms.net. (2017, May 6). *The joy of herb gardening.* Surreyfarms. https://surreyfarms.net/2017/05/06/the-joy-of-herb-gardening/

Sutton, A. L. (2010). *Complementary and alternative medicine sourcebook.* Omnigraphics.

Talerico, D. (2023, February 22). *How to make salve or balms 101: Simple flexible recipe.* Homestead

and Chill. https://homesteadandchill.com/
make-salve-or-balms-recipe-101/

Tammy. (2017, April 12). *10 Engaging ways to create timelines*. The Owl Teacher. https://theowlteacher.com/10-different-timelines/

Teja, P. K, Mithiya, J., Kate, A. S, Bairwa, K, & Chauthe, S. K. (2021). Herbal nanomedicines: Recent advancements, challenges, opportunities and regulatory overview. *Phytomedicine*, 153890. https://doi.org/10.1016/j.phymed.2021.153890

10 Plants to help support immune function. (2023, September 21). Goldthread Tonics. https://drinkgoldthread.com/blogs/plants-with-benefits/10-plants-to-help-support-immune-function

Thangsuk, P., Pinyopornpanish, K., Jiraporncharoen, W., Buawangpong, N., & Angkurawaranon, C. (2021). Is the association between herbal use and blood-pressure control mediated by medication adherence? A cross-sectional study in primary care. *International Journal of Environmental Research and Public Health*, *18*(24), 12916. https://doi.org/10.3390/ijerph182412916

The best places to purchase herbs and supplies world-wide. (2019, August 22). Herbal Academy. https://theherbalacademy.com/purchase-herbs-and-supplies-world-wide/

The history of herbal medicine. (2020, September 28). New Chapter. https://www.newchapter.com/wellness-blog/the-history-of-herbal-medicine/

The history of herbs and herbal medicine. (2014). Planet Natural. https://www.planetnatural.com/herb-gardening-guru/history/

Theodoridis, S., Drakou, E. G., Hickler, T., Thines, M., & Nogues-Bravo, D. (2023). Evaluating natural medicinal resources and their exposure to global change. *The Lancet Planetary Health*, 7(2), e155–e163. https://doi.org/10.1016/ S2542-5196(22)00317-5

These 7 herbs and spices can save your skin. (n.d.). Everyday Health. https://www.everydayhealth. com/beauty-pictures/these-herbs-and-spices-can-save-your-skin.aspx

Thomas, C. (2020, April 19). *15 medicinal herbs to grow and their common uses.* Homesteading Family. https://homesteadingfamily. com/15-medicinal-herbs-to-grow/

Tips for making herbal tea. (2023, March 24). TeaTime. https://teatimemagazine.com/ tips-for-making-herbal-tea/

Tulunay, M., Aypak, C., Yikilkan, H., & Gorpelioglu, S. (2015). Herbal medicine use among Turkish patients with chronic diseases. *Journal of Intercultural Ethnopharmacology*, 4(3), 217. https:// doi.org/10.5455/jice.20150623090040

Vachon, P. (2023, February 21). *How to store and preserve fresh herbs.* CNET. https://www. cnet.com/home/kitchen-and-household/ how-to-store-and-preserve-fresh-herbs/

Walker, J. (2021). *A witch's guide to wildcraft.* Llewellyn Worldwide.

Whelan, J. S., & Dvorkin, L. (2006). Plants from many healing landscapes: Gathering information and teaching clinicians about the cultural use of medicinal herbs. *Journal of the Medical Library Association*, 94(2), 223–226. https://www.ncbi.nlm. nih.gov/pmc/articles/PMC1435855/

White, K. (2015, November 16). *12 Unusual and interesting uses for herbs.* The Herb

Exchange. https://theherbexchange. com/12-unusual-and-interesting-uses-for-herbs/

White, K. (n.d.). *11 Unusual and interesting uses for herbs*. THRIVE. https://www.thrivemagazine.com/single-post/2019/02/22/11-unusual-and-interesting-uses-for-herbs

WholisticMatters. (2020, October 20). *Herbs for children - Safe dosing and indications*. https://wholisticmatters. com/herbs-for-children/

Wild, S. (2023). *Human origins*. Michael O'Mara Books.

Wildcrafting basics: Ethical wildcrafting. (2017, April 17). The School of Forest Medicine. https://forestmedicine.net/ ecological-intelligence-blog/2017/4/10/ ethical-wildcrafting

Wong, C. (2022, March 4). *What herbs can you take for natural pain relief?* Verywell Health. https://www.verywellhealth.com/ herbs-for-pain-management-89299

Yarnell, E. (2015, December 1). *Synergy in herbal medicines*. Association for the Advancement of Restorative Medicine. https://restorativemedicine. org/journal/synergy-in-herbal-medicines-part-1/

Yelton, N. (n.d.). *How to use ginger for gut health*. Nikki Yelton RD. https://nikkiyeltonrd.com/ how-to-use-ginger-for-gut-health/

Yu, S., Chao, Z., & Xiaodong, L. (2020). Traditional medicine in India. *Journal of Traditional Chinese Medical Sciences*, *8*(1). https://doi.org/10.1016/j. jtcms.2020.06.007

Yuan, H., Ma, Q., Ye, L., & Piao, G. (2016). The traditional medicine and modern medicine from natural products. *Molecules*, *21(5),* 559. https://doi. org/10.3390/molecules21050559

Zhang, A. L., Xue, C. C., & Fong, H. (2011). *Integration of herbal medicine into evidence-based clinical practice.* NIH. https://www.ncbi.nlm.nih.gov/books/ NBK92760/

.

www.ingramcontent.com/pod-product-compliance
Lightning Source LLC
Chambersburg PA
CBHW021619270326
41931CB00008B/780